Santa Clara County Free Library

REFERENCE

ERS USED IN LAVA BEDS
L MONUMENT AND
VICINITY.

Emigrant Crossing
Lake Wild Life Refuge
Army Headquarters
m's Graveyard
re Chimneys
Massacre
imneys
ve
te
ater
Below]

CAPTAIN JACK, MODOC RENEGADE

CAPTAIN JACK,
MODOC RENEGADE

By

DORIS PALMER PAYNE

1958

BINFORD & MORT, Publishers
SUCCESSORS TO
METROPOLITAN PRESS, PUBLISHERS
PORTLAND, OREGON

TO

F. A. P.

COLLECTOR OF MODOC ARTIFACTS,
LOVER OF INDIAN LORE

PREFACE

WITHIN the memory of men still living, some of these states of ours, which now seem so united and enduring, were still to be born. From the raw wilderness and their ancient occupants, they were yet to be wrested.

Many and bitter were the struggles between white men and red men for supremacy. The Indians fought obstinately to retain possession of their age-old homes, the pioneers to obtain possession of new ones.

How full those days were with the stuff of which red-blooded life is made . . . with victory and defeat, humor and tragedy! Yet how often these have been lost in the barren desert of purely historical treatment.

The struggle between the Modoc Indians and the onward sweep of civilization . . . incredibly costly in lives and greenbacks . . . . was one of the last and most stubborn of all. As such, it deserves to be recorded in glowing language which makes it vividly real to those of us today who blindly take for granted these United States in which we live.

Every effort has been made to make the story conform to the facts of history. That has not been easy. The very human tendency of original narrators to try to make a good story better and their own exploits more laudable, in addition to the scarcity of authentic records in those days, present serious obstacles to absolute accuracy. Nevertheless, the author has conscientiously striven toward that end, attempting, throughout, to remain unprejudiced and let facts speak for themselves.

It should be of interest that the Lava Beds, the chief setting of this story, have been considered of such outstanding historical importance and fascinating geological formation that they were set aside by President Calvin Coolidge, in 1925, as a National Monument.

The old battle grounds remain practically intact: Captain Jack's stronghold, the man-made fortifications. the sites of the peace commission and Black Ledge massacres and the indescribable terrain. Occasional discoveries of old guns, bullets, buttons from army uniforms and other relics of war, still give eloquent testimony to the bitter struggle of the Modocs in defense of their homes.

Acknowledgment and grateful appreciation are due several "old-timers" for giving the writer many first-hand word pictures of various incidents of the war, and those others who made valuable records available.

D. P.

CONTENTS

PROLOGUE

MANY winters before the great war with the white men, the Modoc braves sat in solemn council. Their Chief searched the faces before him in the firelight. At last he spoke.

"I am Chief of the Modocs. My people are few. The palefaces are many. They hunt us as they would the antelope. Shall we do nothing but bleat like sick sheep? The Great Spirit gave us this country. I say let us fight for it! I am not afraid to die. I will not run. I will die with my bow in my hand! Let them see their own people food for buzzards. I have spoken. Now let others speak."

A boy rose from the circle of braves. Kientepoos, son of the Chief, folded his arms across his chest as he had seen his father do. With great dignity, he spoke.

"I am a Modoc. I am not afraid of the palefaces. But we do wrong to kill them. They do not know we are Modocs. They kill our people for wrongs other tribes have done them. They are many, like grass on the hillsides. We cannot kill them all. More will come. If we fight them, they will not rest until all Modocs are dead. I say, let us make peace with the white man."

The Chief looked proudly at his son. "My people,"

he said, "you have heard the words of Kientepoos. He is but a boy, too young to fight. But he has spoken forth bravely. I see in him a great leader of my people."

CHAPTER I

PALEFACE TREACHERY

THE Indians, their cinnamon-hued faces and half-naked bodies blending with the lava rock of the high plain, moved on silent, moccasined feet from sagebrush to juniper in perfect concealment. Their prominent cheek bones were smeared with war-paint, and their eyes—narrow slits in faces marked with noses straight as the Grecian—lost not a single movement of the train of covered wagons clattering along an ill-defined trail its occupants entirely unaware of lurking danger.

In strong contrast, the sixty-five men, women and children, enveloped in a cloud of dust from the high-bowed, canvas-covered wagons drawn by jaded oxen and raw-boned horses, were impelled by a buoyant sense of relief from the intense anxiety of the days just past, for they had left behind them the hostile Snake and Pit river Indians. Before them lay the goal toward which so many weary and heart-rending miles had led them . . . Oregon, the promised land.

Although they had, indeed, left the Snake and the Pit river tribes behind, the bitter animosity of these

Indians was even now incarnate in the Modoc redskins, stalking their trail. Preceding the fall of 1852, these Modoc Indians had been friendly with the white men who had passed through their country, for they liked the gifts of flour, coffee and tobacco received from them. But now their attitude had been completely changed by the misunderstanding of the identity of the three tribes on the part of another emigrant party.

The trouble had begun when the Snakes, always the terror of white men passing through their country, had stolen horses belonging to a party of westward travelers. These animals were sold or bartered to the Pit river Indians, who in turn traded them off to the Modocs. Not knowing one tribe from the other, the original owners of the horses found them in possession of the Modocs and, in recapturing their property, killed braves of that tribe and captured a few of their squaws.

Never having done the white men any wrong, the Chief of the Modocs was incensed at the death of his men and what he considered stealing of his rightful property. He vowed revenge. It mattered little to him that the particular group singled out for his purpose, was innocent of any connection with the trouble which had sent him and his braves on the warpath. Just as Indians had been Indians to the owners of these horses, so were white men white men to the Modocs. They were all invaders coming to take the lives and lands of Modoc braves; to steal their horses, make slaves of their women.

Crouched low behind sagebrush, the Chief turned over in his mind the wrongs which had been done him and, filled with a grim satisfaction unbetrayed by his stolid features, he watched his prey advance unsuspectingly into the trap he had set. It was the satisfaction of a man who has carefully laid his plans for revenge, bided his time patiently and is about to strike the blow which will compensate for what he has suffered in the past.

Like a long snake wriggling across the plain, the wagon-train approached the place where the trail dropped abruptly from the plateau. The women and the children were riding, happy now with anticipation; the men, most of them, plodding along on foot. A few men, however, were on horseback, scouting out the trail. Suddenly one of the scouts waved his hat in the air and galloped back to the wagons, shouting the news that a large lake lay just ahead.

As the rest of the party came up, they gazed out upon a body of water which stretched for miles, an unrippled, iridescent expanse, lighted by the sunset glow, banked on the far side by low, brownish-yellow hills. Joyful shouts echoed from wagon to wagon as mothers called their children and pointed with exultation to evidence that their dreams were fast coming true.

Yet back in the sagebrush lurked the redskin braves who knew what the white men did not . . . that once on the lake shore, the palefaces would be hemmed in by water on one side and rugged, towering cliffs on the other. There they could be easily slaughtered with no more chance of escape than sheep in a corral.

The men urged the horses and oxen on, the clumsy wagon wheels clattering, brakes grinding, down the steep road to the lake, then through the shallow water to a fairly level stretch of ground which lay between cliffs and shore. Here they prepared to camp for the night which was almost upon them.

Above, the Indians slipped stealthily from rock to rock, ever nearer. When they had advanced as close as caution would allow, they were near enough to see the weather-etched faces of the sturdy white men who had suffered life-threatening hardships in pursuit of their dreams of land and homes. Hostile eyes watched them as they began to unhitch the weary animals from the loose-jointed wagons and turn them loose to graze; hostile ears listened as the palefaces whistled about their work for the first time in weeks.

The redskins held themselves in check while the fire was built and the women began preparation of the evening meal. The boys and girls ran here and there. Some of them delightedly dabbled their dusty toes in the lapping lake water, others came within a stone's throw of the Indians as they helped gather sagebrush and greasewood for the fire.

Darkness had fallen by the time the meagre meal was ready. The chill of September had touched the air making the warmth of the fire doubly welcome to those who gathered around it, laughing and talking of what lay ahead. An armful of wood, tossed on the fire to provide light while they ate, caused flames to dart high into the air, sending weird shadows careening among the group, who moved about or lounged on the ground as their interests dictated.

The Indians were becoming restless waiting for the signal of attack from their Chief. Taut bows with arrows nocked were held ready to draw. Some let their hands slip to the glistening black obsidian knife blades at their belts, making sure they were in readiness.

A shrill whoop! The whir of an arrow and a bedlam of war cries shattered the night. Arrows seared their way with deadly aim straight for their firelit targets. The men, first to be picked off, shouted futile warnings to the women and children, staggered, cursed and fell most of them being killed or wounded by the first flight of poisoned, black-tipped shafts.

As the Indians swarmed down from the rocks, their high-pitched yells mingled with the shrieks of women and the terror-filled cries of children. A few guns barked defiance but their echoes only mocked those who had pulled the triggers. One or two of the men who had survived the first onslaught grappled with the attackers, with death the lot of the loser. Panic-stricken, some of the women and children ran into the water of the lake, only to be drowned or snatched back and scalped alive.

As suddenly as the attack began, it was over. Gory scalps dripped from the belts of the Indians, dead bodies reddened the ground with their blood but the Indians were not through. Fresh fuel sent the flames leaping higher to light the way for pillaging and looting. The redskins, fevered with victory, clambered into the wagons, stripping them bare of everything that took their fancy.

This done, several braves snatched flaming brands from the fire and ran from wagon to wagon, whooping and yelling wildly, as they touched off the canvas tops. Soon every wagon was ablaze, crackling and hissing, as reflections of the flames on the water danced crazily and great plumes of smoke rose into the still air.

Returning to their camp, the Indians held a great celebration, alternately boasting and quarreling over their prowess and the booty they had taken, which included horses and oxen. It was a moonless night, but the light from the council fire showed the dim outlines of their lodges, peculiarly built of matting woven of tule rushes, placed over a framework of willow poles and plastered on the outside with mud.

At the edge of the camp, a fringe of willows and the low sound of running water marked the place where Lost river slipped along on its unhurried way to Tule lake. Crowding in on the camp from the other three sides were tall sagebrush and bitterbrush, while in the distance a broken skyline showed the camp to be in a valley surrounded by mountainous country.

The braves who gathered around the fire were clad in buckskin shirts with leggings and moccasins made of woven tules or deerhide. They were lean, muscular men with straight, black hair and beardless faces, hideously smeared with war paint. Back and forth went the talk among them, now jocular, now serious but always in the heavy guttural of the Modoc tongue.

Squaws, most of them shorter than the men and stockily built, moved about the camp carrying arm loads of sagebrush and juniper for the fire or tending to the needs of the children. They, too, wore buckskin clothing with tule baskets fitted snugly on their heads.

Sitting just outside the circle of braves around the fire was a small boy, some twelve or fourteen years old. He seemed to take more interest in the councils of his elders than the other children, as indeed he might, for he was destined one day to become leader of the Modocs. Born near this very spot, Kientepoos, for such was his Indian name, cherished a deep love for his home country, yet seemed to have a remarkable intuition for one so young, which told him that the way to retain it was to make friends with the white men and not to fight them. Before the massacre of these emigrants, he had tried to restrain his father, Chief of the tribe, from taking vengeance on the palefaces, but he might as well have tried to blow away the clouds with his breath.

Here he sat, listening gravely, although he refused to

take part in the celebration, for he knew in his heart that the white men would avenge what his father and his braves had done. As he sat cross-legged, the firelight revealing a broad, intelligent forehead, bright, deep-set eyes and strong mouth and chin, he thought not only of what the future might bring, but of what he had been told of the great past of the Modocs.

Only the day before, one of the old men of the tribe had said to him, "You, Kientepoos, will be Chief after many moons. You must learn much and forget nothing. We have not always been Modocs. At one time our band belonged to the powerful tribe of Lalacas. We did our share in all things. Our braves fought in the battles against enemy tribes. We provided supplies of fish from Lost river; deer, bear and antelope meat; camas roots and wocus seed.

"But the head Chief of all the Lalacas demanded more and more until we had little left for ourselves. One day Moadocus, head man of our band, called a council and said we must no longer send the Chief of the Lalacas all the things he demanded. We declared we would be free. We would not submit to being made slaves. We threw away our allegiance to the head Chief of the Lalacas.

"Many battles were fought, many brave warriors were killed. But at last we defeated the Lalacas, now known as Klamaths. We are the Lost river tribe that defeated the great Lalacas. We are Modocs!"

Kientepoos pondered these things and wondered what the outcome of the night's activities might be as the fire died down to embers and the braves began to drift off to their lodges. At last Kientepoos, too, went to his bed of woven tule matting, but he lay awake for a long time listening to the night-sounds and juggling the confused impressions which crowded into his young head.

On the morning following the massacre of the emigrants, the Indians were up with the sun. The bucks separated into small parties, some hunting with their obsidian-tipped arrows on the wooded mountain slopes nearby, others fishing in Lost river with nets and long spears or poles tipped with blades finely chipped from black volcanic glass. The squaws went about their tasks of dressing hides for winter clothing, weaving baskets and moccasins, grinding the seed of the wocus for flour and digging camas roots with sharp pointed sticks.

Meanwhile, unknown to the Modocs, some of the emigrants had escaped and made their way to Yreka. California, a mining settlement some seventy miles southwest. The story of the gruesome tragedy leapt from lip to lip and sent public feeling to such a fever pitch that a group of settlers and miners determined immediately to take up the cause of the murdered white men and exterminate the Indians who had so fiendishly slaughtered them.

These frontiersmen, about forty strong, chose Ben Wright, a rugged, weather-scarred miner as their leader and, in short order, they were on their way to the scene of the butchery, mounted on the best horses obtainable and well outfitted with plenty of supplies. Across a range of timbered mountains and miles of sagebrush-covered valleys they rode, arriving at the spot where the ill-fated emigrants had camped, four days after the slaughter.

Hardened as these men were to raw realities of frontier life, they were unprepared for what they saw. As they dismounted, the men took off their hats and stood with heads bowed, gazing at a scene too grisly for even the stoutest hearted to witness without emotion. The Indians had left the bodies of the victims where they had fallen, to become the prey of coyotes and scavengers. There, before them, lay the evidence of pillage, surrounded by charred ruins of the wagons.

Silently, with tears streaming unashamedly down their tanned and bearded faces, the men set about digging a trench into which they placed the bodies side by side and covered them over with soil and rocks.

These last rites performed for their countrymen, the party held a conference to decide what their next step would be. To these men, Indian hunting had always been more or less of a sport, but now it became serious business. Some were for locating the Modoc camp and attacking it that very night. Others contended that such a plan involved too much risk, for they knew the Indians, when banded together, were ferocious fighters. They finally agreed that it would be wiser to proceed cautiously, catch them a few at a time while they were hunting or fishing and pick them off from ambush with their rifles.

But Ben Wright disapproved both of these plans and made a suggestion of his own. While still in Yreka, he had obtained a supply of strychnine from a druggist, allegedly for the purpose of poisoning coyotes. Even now it was tucked away in his saddle bag. Why not pretend to be friendly with these Indians, arrange for a big peace feast and then put the poison in the food? This would accomplish their purpose with the least risk to the white men, who could then scalp their dead victims and be hailed as heroes by the folks back home. This idea appealed to the men, who much preferred to return home victorious rather than to fall victims of Indian arrows themselves, and so the plan was agreed upon.

When Ben Wright and a few of his men came upon a couple of Modocs out hunting the next day, they told one of them who could understand a little "white-man-talk" that they were friends of the Indians, backing up their words and signs with gifts of food from their saddle bags. The Great White Father back in Washington, Ben Wright said, had sent him to the Modocs to make peace with them. He had brought much food and if these Indians would gather their tribesmen together they would have a big feast and bury the hatchet.

The Indians who had talked with Wright returned to their camp and told the others that they had, at last, found a white man with many followers who wanted to be their friends. Having lived in anxiety and fear of what the white men's vengeance might be, most of the Modocs were eager to make peace, so riders on ponies set out to gather in the tribesmen from their pursuit of game and fish to be present at the proposed feast and peace council.

Meanwhile, Ben Wright and his men pitched their tents on a little knoll just above, and very near, the Indian camp which was sandwiched in between them and the north bank of Lost river. During the day, Wright went about among the braves and their families, bestowing his genial smile here, a trinket there, until the Indians were, for the most part, entirely disarmed by his friendly manner. He suggested that they hold the big feast and council fire at the white men's camp where they would be better protected from the cold wind and the rain that had drizzled disagreeably throughout the day.

The Indians agreed, but a few of them were not taken in by all this display of friendliness. Some of these skeptics sought the opinion of an older sub-chief

of the tribe, Schonchin by name, who had the reputation
for shrewdness. They had found him seated cross-
legged in the shade of a juniper tree, chipping out
hunting arrows from a crude piece of the glistening volcanic rock with a deer horn tool.

When the question was put, Schonchin remained silent for a few moments. His deeply lined face was as
inscrutable as a piece of parchment and his powerfully-
knit body swayed slightly as he worked. Then he shook
his gray head solemnly. "Paleface talk too good, promise too much. Peace food maybe bait for Indians," he
said cryptically . . . and went on with his chipping. The
Chief, himself, had put it into plainer words, warning
his people not to touch the food until white men had
eaten.

As the time set for the peace talk drew near, Schonchin and a few other braves were not among the fifty
bucks who gathered around the huge fire Wright's men
had built. Those who had been unable to resist the
prospect of a feast squatted on their heels or sat on tule
mats, their bows unstrung at their sides.

When everything was ready, Ben Wright urged the
Modocs to make merry over the food so that everyone
would be in good humor for the talk that was to follow.
Mindful of their Chief's warning, however, the Indians
waited impatiently for the white men to begin and gave
first one excuse and then another to put off partaking
of the feast.

Ben Wright rose and approached the Chief, asking
him why the braves were waiting. The Chief stood
up and faced Wright, fearlessly. Through an interpreter who knew a little English, he told Wright that the
Indians would not touch food before their hosts had
done so.

In a flash, Wright realized that his scheme to poison them had failed. He smiled grimly and told the chief that if his braves wouldn't eat the food they could eat dust. With that, he whipped out his pistol, pressed it to the defenseless Chief's heart and pulled the trigger. Instantly, Wright's men opened fire upon their unarmed guests, mowing them down before they could begin to get their unstrung bows and arrows into action.

Within five minutes, forty-one braves lay dead or dying with not one white man so much as scratched. Wright's men drew jack-knives from their pockets, and within sight of the squaws and children, who came running at the sound of the shots and yells, they began the ghastly business of obtaining scalps for their shot pouches to provide their friends with evidence of their prowess.

Not waiting until morning, Wright gave orders to break up camp, so amid the wails and shrieks of squaws, the white men headed back to Yreka, leaving only five of the Indians who had attended their "peace" conference alive and all of those wounded.

Decorated with the scalps of their victims, Ben Wright and his Indian hunters rode into Yreka to find themselves the heroes of the day. In celebrating the success of the expedition*, a great dance was given attended by all the townspeople and miners within miles, who showered Wright with congratulations and hailed him the "great civilizer".

(* Note: There seem to be as many differing versions of the "Ben Wright affair" as there are accounts of it. The one given here is used because it gives the most logical basis for the undisputed conviction later held by the Indians that they had been treacherously attacked by the white men during what had been represented as a "peace talk." It was this conviction which twenty years later made the Modocs so distrustful of the efforts of the peace commission.

CHAPTER II

SAVED BY A WOMAN'S WIT

ALL night long the wails of lamentation continued in the Modoc camp on the banks of Lost river, the cries of the children mingling with those of their mothers. The few braves who remained alive mounted ponies, even before dawn began to bring out the colors in the brown and green hills, and were off to spread the news to others of their tribe that their Chief and forty braves had been treacherously shot down in the "peace talk" that had promised so much.

As soon as daylight permitted, the squaws began their sad task of gathering up the dead. All day they searched, but by nightfall, they were able to find few more than half of those who were missing, the rest having sunk to the muddy bottom of Lost river where they had been shot in trying to escape by swimming across.

Meanwhile, great piles of wood were gathered in by the children, among them Kientepoos, who was grave but stoical, over the death of his father. Under the direction of the medicine man, a large funeral pyre was built and the bodies cremated with impressive ceremony which lasted all through the night.

For a week, other members of the tribe, those who had been called from their hunting and fishing by news of the great tragedy, continued to arrive. Over and over again, the story of the horror-filled night was told until everyone knew the smallest detail by heart . . . until the survivors had it etched deeply in their minds.

After a large number of the Modocs had gathered, they assembled in council to decide who should take the place of their dead Chief. Many and long were the arguments, for it was a serious matter. Some maintained that Kientepoos, son of the Chief, was their rightful leader, while others declared he was too young, that the band needed an older, wiser head.

The dissenting faction accused others of wanting Kientepoos as Chief so they could dominate him and run things to suit themselves. This group claimed the chieftainship should go to the old man, Schonchin, who could lead them wisely because of his age and broader experience. They pointed to his skill as a hunter, his influence in council and his determined hostility to the palefaces' invasion of their country.

Meanwhile Kientepoos sat silently listening, his dreams of becoming Chief growing bright and dim by turns as his elders argued the question, yet feeling that if he were given the chance, he could make a good leader for his people. In spite of the shock of his father's death at the white men's hands, he still desired to live at peace with them, for he realized the futility of combatting their unlimited numbers and great power. To fight them, he felt sure, would mean the extermination of his tribesmen who were, in comparison to the white men, so few and so poorly armed.

When the decision that old Schonchin should be their chief was finally announced, Kientepoos gulped down his disappointment and said nothing. Yet the dream long nurtured in his heart only grew stronger and he determined that some day he would make it come true.

But in this ambition, Kientepoos was not alone. He had a formidable rival in Chief Schonchin's younger brother, later known among the white men as Schonchin John. Both of them were head men of the tribe under the new regime, which gave them ample occasion to come into conflict with each other. As the years passed and Chief Schonchin's advancing age rendered him less and less active in the affairs of the tribe, the actual leadership divided itself between the two younger men, each ambitious for the chieftainship, each having his own staunch supporters.

By the time Kientepoos had grown up to young manhood, he had won for himself a place of respect among members of his tribe, and the friendship of several white men of prominence in the mining town of Yreka. Lithe and wiry, carrying about 160 pounds on his stocky frame, he made a fine impression among the frontiersmen. His high cheek bones were prominent features of his broad, bronzed face, lighted by a fine pair of dark eyes, which inspired confidence by their steady gaze.

Schonchin John, although older than Kientepoos by several years, was similar in build with somewhat irregular features marked by a strong chin. In disposition, he was the exact opposite of his even-tempered, reserved rival, being stormily hot-tempered and bitterly hostile toward the whites, avoiding contact with them whenever he could.

That was not always possible, however, for in the years that followed the Bloody Point massacre and the Ben Wright affair, as these two events came to be known, the Modoc country was the goal of more and more settlers, chiefly stockmen. The Modocs, through the influence of Kientepoos, managed to stay on fairly friendly terms with them, while the braves, led by Schonchin John, were engaged in many battles with neighboring tribes located chiefly in the vicinity of Klamath lake, Klamath river, Pit river and Mt. Shasta.

During this time, all of these tribes were more or less under the influence of Esquire Elisha Steele, a lawyer of Yreka, who had been made acting Indian superintendent for northern California. Steele, who had crossed the plains to California in 1859, had always been dominated by a desire to see justice done at all times and he was trained by years of experience among different tribes to understand their point of view. He often had championed fair play, dealing out punishment where it was deserved, be it to white man or Indian.

Kientepoos made many trips to Yreka, and regarded the thin-faced, black-bearded lawyer as his friend to whom he could turn with confidence. Elisha Steele liked the young Modoc sub-chief because he had always shown himself inclined toward peace and because, as Steele himself said, "I have never known him to take a glass af liquor and I have known him to whip his men for doing so."

One spring day in 1864, Steele, upon returning from San Francisco, found the lot adjoining his house swarming with several hundred Indians. Kientepoos and a large delegation of Modocs were among them. Representatives of five or six tribes were waiting for the superintendent's arrival.

Steele learned that his wife had been talking to these redskins, telling them how they could best get along with each other and with the white people. He was not surprised, therefore, when they expressed themselves as willing to enter into treaties with each other to put a stop to their quarrels.

After two days of negotiations, they were so well pleased with the results that when Kientepoos proposed to have Steele made the "Big Chief" of all the tribes, a great shout of approval rose from the crowd. In keeping with this decision it was also agreed that any difficulty arising among the Indians should be submitted to Steele, whose decision should be final.

During the two days of council an election was held by the Modocs present by which they renounced Old Schonchin as their Chief and chose Kientepoos to take his place. Steele recognized the young Chief, as such and dubbed him "Captain Jack" on account of his resemblance to a miner by that name. The name stuck. and he was henceforth "Captain Jack" to white men and Indians alike.

The treaty itself, to which a number of townspeople were witnesses, dealt chiefly with the localities which the different tribes could rightfully claim as their own, and contained an agreement that, thereafter, they were to live in peace with each other and with the whites. It was quite informal in its nature, never being officially authorized nor ratified by the government.

Kientepoos, recognized at last as Chief and proudly bearing his new title, "Captain Jack," returned to his Lost river country enthusiastic over the prospects which the future promised. Surely now, he thought, his tribe could go about their hunting and fishing undisturbed

... and so they did for a short time. But it was too good to last.

As the West became more and more thickly populated, the government began to take steps to make more land available for white men by placing the Indians on reservations. The Superintendent of Indian Affairs for Oregon was instructed in the summer of 1864 to "negotiate a treaty with all the Indians in the Klamath country, including the Modocs".

Accordingly, a council was held in October at a place since known as Council Grove. Here, among the pines which lined the lapping waters of Upper Klamath lake, the Chief and sub-chiefs of each tribe gathered. Much to Captain Jack's chagrin, he found that the Oregon superintendent refused to recognize him as Chief of the Modocs as Elisha Steele had done. He recognized old Chief Schonchin as leader of the Modocs. The combined efforts of Captain Jack's friends were none too much to prevent him from bolting the council then and there.

The articles of the agreement, as they were finally drawn up after several days of negotiations, set aside a large tract of land, none of which was occupied by the Modocs, to be known as the Klamath reservation. This was to be the joint home of the Klamaths and Modocs. All the other territory occupied by the two tribes was to be ceded to the United States on condition that certain acts be performed by the government in a specified time.

If Captain Jack was irate at first, he was more than rebellious now. Worse than injury to his personal pride was the humiliation he felt for the Modocs having to give up their home country and live like mere tenants on land traditionally claimed by their ancient enemies, the Klamaths. He also resented the idea of having his people regulated by government officials. Accustomed to complete freedom, the clothing, equipment and provisions promised by the government were inadequate compensation for loss of liberty.

Captain Jack maintained that he was satisfied with the treaty he had made with Esquire Steele of Yreka and refused to believe it was ineffective, as the government representatives pointed out, because the Lost river country lay in Oregon instead of California. State lines meant nothing to him, and, indeed, they had only recently been defined by white men.

In view of all these facts, it took a host of rosy promises and considerable pressure to induce Captain Jack to sign the treaty. Even so, he placed his mark under his Indian name, Kientepoos, with grudging reluctance.

Dissatisfaction with reservation life grew steadily among the Modocs, and it wasn't long until the spirit of rebellion flared up among many of the prouder and more spirited braves, giving Captain Jack an opportunity to recruit enough followers to justify an attempt to break away from the reservation. With their backing, he determined to take the course which would enable him to regain the realization of his life-long dream of chieftainship.

He chose a dark, moonless night on which to rally the rebellious followers and slip away unseen. Next morning, fifty braves and their families once more occupied the old Modoc village on Lost river.

But if these braves thought their troubles were now over, they were promptly disillusioned. The settlers, having laid full claim to the land outside the reservation, resented the presence of the Indians and complained to the government, in many cases making false accusations to strengthen their appeal.

Spurred by repeated urging, the reservation authorities made three different attempts to induce the renegade band to return to the reservation, but in each case without success. Captain Jack, although continually harassed, maintained he was living strictly in accordance with the Yreka treaty and for five years he defied all efforts to drive him onto Klamath land. Then things began to happen.

In 1869 a young army captain. O. C. Knapp, was Indian agent on the reservation. His experience in handling redskins, except at the point of a gun, was decidedly limited and he had little patience with the peaceful efforts that had been made. Moreover, rumors to the effect that the success of Captain Jack's band in defying the government was producing a rebellious spirit among the other Indians of the reservation, prompted him to urge the government authorities to resort to force.

They had about come to the conclusion that military coercion was the only alternative, when A. B. Meacham took office as the new Superintendent of Indian Affairs for Oregon and convinced them to let him make one more peaceable attempt to bring in the renegade band.

Meacham's reputation for fearlessness and fairmindedness in dealing with Indians during the twenty-five years he had been associated with them in Iowa and elsewhere, had preceded him, and Knapp was impressed on being advised that the new superintendent would handle the situation in person.

On the day that Meacham was to arrive with the wagon bringing in supplies, Knapp arranged to meet him with proper ceremony. He had his side whiskers

Captain Jack, Modoc Chief

Old Chief Schonchin, Modoc Indian

(Photo by Signal Corps, U. S. Army)

and mustache trimmed, his chin smoothly shaved and his uniform meticulously cleaned and pressed for the occasion.

The expectations of the spruce young officer suffered quite a shock as he caught his first glimpse of Meacham sitting alongside the driver on the wagon seat smoking an old pipe. What he saw was a stocky, well-knit frame supporting a partially bald head. The most striking thing about the man was the squareness of his jaw, accentuated by side-whiskers and moustache, now badly in need of trimming, into which a few gray hairs had found their way. Aside from this, there was little to fulfill the glorified idea of his superior which Knapp had formulated in his mind. Why, even the man's trousers were baggy at the knees!

Meacham liked the young captain for his concise, straight-forward manner, but soon realized his limitations as an Indian agent. During the conversations between them, Meacham tried to investigate every angle of the problem Captain Jack presented, and more and more he became aware of the definitely condescending attitude Knapp held toward his charges, as if they were no more to him than bothersome children in need of discipline.

Knapp tried to hold out for drastic use of military force, but found Meacham stubbornly determined to avoid such a policy if at all possible. Finally, Knapp was forced to agree to cooperate with him.

Accordingly, they dispatched a courier with a message to the rebel Chief, asking him to meet them at Linkville, a small settlement of square-front stores and scattered cabins, which had arisen on the east bank of Link river to serve the growing needs of the settlers. But Captain Jack was well aware of the antagonism these people held toward him and replied that if the superintendent insisted on seeing him, he would have to come to his Lost river country.

This made Meacham and Knapp more determined than ever to bring Captain Jack and his band back on the reservation before they became more obstinate in asserting their independence. They decided to accept his terms, but not until they assured themselves of the protection of a small detachment of troops from Fort Klamath, which was a military outpost established a short time before to insure the security of the settlers.

The party which set out for Captain Jack's Lost river camp consisted of a small squad of soldiers, Meacham and Knapp, two other government officers and several guides, interpreters and teamsters. They left Klamath Agency on horseback one December morning and covered the distance of some forty-five miles to Linkville at a good clip. There, they left the teams with their supplies to follow them next morning and ordered the soldiers to remain in Linkville to await further instructions.

From the settlement, the eleven remaining members of the party picked their way across a sagebrush-covered valley along the west bank of Lost river. When within a short distance of the Modoc camp, they saw a cloud of dust approaching, which soon revealed four Indians mounted on ponies. As the redskins drew near, they formed four abreast across the trail and halted Meacham's men with the command, "Kaw-tuk! (Stop!)"

For a moment, no one spoke. Each party was obviously gauging the strength of the other. The white men observed that the Indians were armed about as well as they were themselves, each man with a rifle and a revolver.

One of the Indians broke the silence, demanding in

broken English to know what business brought the palefaces there. Meacham replied that he wanted to talk to their Chief. The answer was instant and determined. "Him no talk. Him got no business with white man. You go back!"

But Meacham was stubborn. He didn't intend to be defied, intimidated or eluded as the other government officers had been. These Indians, he felt sure, would respect the superior numbers of his party if it came to a show-down. On the strength of this, he refused to be bluffed, although he knew it meant taking desperate chances. He barked an order to the others who put spurs to their horses, pushing past the Indians at a gallop. The four Indians wheeled their ponies and in spite of the handicap of a slow start, they soon passed Meacham's party and kept the lead in a breathless four mile race to the Modoc camp. While still several hundred yards away, the white men saw the Indians leap from their ponies, run up a rude stairway, leading to the entrance of the largest lodge, and disappear.

The men reined up their sweating horses in a camp that appeared deserted, except for a few squaws and children who ignored their presence. Although the circumstances were ominous, they at least had a few minutes to get their bearings.

The lodges, of which there were thirteen in the village, looked to be little more than mounds of earth with an open slit across the top, which served as window, door and chimney. In the near distance, the newly made state line markers could be seen.

As no one appeared, Meacham, followed by the others, started toward the lodge into which the four Indians had disappeared. The only means of entrance was by way of steps cut in the earthen roof leading to the rectangular opening on top. Up these steps Meacham had begun to climb when an Indian suddenly appeared from within and commanded tersely, "One man come! No more!"

Since Meacham was in the lead and there was no turning back, he went on to the top of the lodge and looked down through the narrow opening. At first it was too dim after the bright sunlight to distinguish anything, but as he climbed down a ladder of heavy rawhide thongs, he saw the eyes of fifty armed braves centered on him.

Intuition and long experience told the superintendent that he dared not retrace his steps or show the slightest indication of the fear he felt. All too conscious of the pounding of his heart, he reached the bottom fully expecting to be met with a shower of bullets and arrows. A clammy sweat broke out on his face, but he advanced toward Captain Jack, who stood apart from the others, and offered his hand. The Chief refused it without so much as a change in facial expression.

Enduring the stare of a hundred eyes, Meacham coolly lighted his pipe in the face of a silence sharp-edged and burning with hatred. The close air, heavy with the combined odors of smoke from the fire, dried fish and crowded human beings, for a moment threatened to overcome him with nausea.

The trapped man was about to risk making a bolt for the open air and his companions when a stern voice broke the silence. The words were addressed to Meacham. "What for you come here? Jack got no business with paleface. You not him ty-ee (chief). Him no want talk. Hal-lu-i-me til-li-cum! (You stranger! You go way!)"

Meacham singled out the speaker who impressed

him as a straight and proud looking brave of medium height, whose beak nose reminded him of a light complexioned Jew. The thing that caught and held his eye, however, was a scar, livid in the firelight, extending from forehead to chin. It was apparent from his bearing and speech that he was one of Captain Jack's head men.

Meacham's throat went dry and words came with difficulty, but, somehow, he managed to make a reply. "I am white man ty-ee," he said slowly and distinctly. "The Great White Father sent me to care for all the Indians, including the Modocs. I have some new things to talk about. Whether you are my friends or not, I am your friend. I have come to see my men, and I want a hearing. I am not afraid to talk, not afraid to hear your Chief talk."

Captain Jack, who had been gazing steadily at Meacham, did not take his eyes from the white man's face until Scarface Charley had finished interpreting his words. Then he moved uneasily and replied in deliberate fashion. The self-appointed interpreter reported Captain Jack as saying, "Tell him Jack has nothing to say paleface ty-ee want to hear. White mans all liars. They all swindlers. What they talk, no can believe. Jack never gave up Lost river country. Palefaces live here, too, all right with Jack. Him no 'fraid to hear paleface talk."

That broke the ice, and with more confidence, Meacham asked the Chief through his head man if his friends might come in. The Chief grudgingly consented, sending one of the braves to summon them. When all were assembled, Captain Jack rummaged around in one corner of the lodge and returned with a parcel of papers which he handed to Meacham.

The superintendent found them to be letters from Steele and other prominent citizens of Yreka. They were in the nature of "passes" used in going to and coming from the little mining settlement. They stated that Captain Jack was a well-disposed Indian; that he wanted the settlers to know he was a friend to the white people and that they had nothing to fear from him.

Meacham wisely treated the letters with respect, his consideration of them causing the Modocs to relax a little in their hostile attitude. Nevertheless, the superintendent thought it best to further gain their confidence and friendship before coming to the point of his visit, so he pointed out that darkness was close at hand and his party, not being able to return to Linkville, would like to be guests of the Modoc Chief for the night.

This display of confidence further softened Captain Jack's attitude and he ordered a camp prepared for his visitors. The council was adjourned to reconvene the next morning.

Meacham and his men watched with great interest as the Indians set about building a temporary lodge. First, they dug small holes in the ground with a sharp pointed tool called a camas stick. It was made of hard manzanita wood with a short bar forming a cross at the upper end and it was generally used by the squaws to dig roots in much the same way that a gardener uses a spade.

Willow poles about eight feet long were inserted into these holes and covered with sheets of woven tule matting. The upper ends of the poles were drawn together to form a roof, the entrance being formed by the poles overlapping at one point. When completed, its shape resembled a large inverted bowl.

A plentiful supply of sagebrush was piled around the camp for fuel, and a large quantity of roots and fresh fish from Lost river were provided for food. The roots weren't so palatable to the white men, but the fish, when baked in the sagebrush embers, more than satisfied their ravenous appetites.

Supper over, Meacham placed one man on guard and the rest spread their saddle blankets on the ground inside their lodge and attempted to sleep. This seemed next to impossible under the circumstances, but at least they tried to give the appearance of sleeping, for they knew it would never do to let the Indians guess they didn't dare to close their eyes.

They were all greatly relieved when morning found them still safe, although stiff and sore from their night on the hard ground. The men's spirits rose considerable when the supply wagon arrived, bringing coffee, beef, flour and other provisions. Knowing there is nothing like a feast to melt a cold-blooded Indian into friendliness, they immediately set about preparing one.

The redskins looked on like children watching preparations for a Thanksgiving dinner, but when at last they were invited to eat they coldly refused. The whites, much chagrined, couldn't understand this attitude until Meacham heard the whisper being passed from brave to brave, "Remember Ben Wright!"

Thereupon, Meacham told his men to "fall to" with a will in order to convince the Indians that everything was all right. After watching the white men, as they ate heartily, the Modocs became reassured and they, too, joined in . . . still apprehensive at first, but finally with their fears laid at rest.

When the last scrap of food had disappeared, everyone seemed in rare good humor, leading Meacham to suggest that a council be called immediately. Captain Jack, however, insisted he would discuss nothing with the white men until the interpreter, for whom he had sent, arrived.

The day had turned off intensely cold, a high wind filling the air with fine sleet, causing the party of white men to wait impatiently in the shelter erected for them. About noon, it was announced that the interpreter had arrived and, for the first time, Meacham was introduced to Winema.

The woman who stood before him was an attractive young full-blooded Modoc, a cousin of the Chief. Born in a village at the upper end of Link river near the sacred lands of the ancient Lalacas, she had earned for herself the title of "Winema", which meant "Woman-Chief-of-the-Brave-Heart". Her marriage to Frank Riddle, a miner, had opened up a new world for her the ways of which she readily learned.

When the council opened in the Chief's big lodge, Winema looked strangely out of place in the gathering of men. She had given up the Indian mode of dress, wearing in its place a plain, full-skirted calico dress, reaching to her ankles, a bright colored shawl thrown about her plump shoulders over which cascaded a wealth of dark brown hair. Meacham thought he had never seen an Indian woman with such an intelligent face or such an assured composure of manner.

The fire burned gustily in the center of the council tent, while Captain Jack and his braves were seated cross-legged on tule mats on one side, and Meacham with his ten companions sat on the other. The Chief, speaking through Winema as interpreter, opened the council, demanding the object of the white men's visit.

Meacham came immediately to the point with the

declaration that they were there for no other purpose than to induce Captain Jack and his people to return to the Klamath reservation. He reminded the Chief of the treaty which he had signed, impressing him with the fact that this was his last chance to return peaceably. If he would not go with them willingly, then soldiers would be sent to force him to go.

Captain Jack, in turn, reminded Meacham of how the promises of the treaty had been broken. He said the pact made at Council Grove was no good, that he was living under an agreement he had made with Steele in Yreka, which was a good treaty. Convinced that he was right in the position he had taken, he showed no signs of capitulating.

Meacham explained to him how the treaty with the Klamath Indians and the government had superseded the Yreka agreement. It took considerable diplomatic skirmishing and even the production of the original paper on which the Chief had made his mark as a sign of acceptance, before Captain Jack showed any indication of weakening.

At last he told Winema to tell the white ty-ee he might go with him if he could live near his friend, Link River Jack. Meacham's assurance that he could have any land not already occupied appeared to settle the matter.

Thinking they had at last won over the rebellious Chief, where so many others had failed, the white men were filled with unrestrained rejoicing which nearly proved their undoing. These innocent demonstrations of triumph over the Modocs, always a proud people, antagonized them beyond reason.

This was especially true of Curly Head Doctor, the Modoc medicine man . . . a tight-lipped, heavy-browed

Indian and one of the few with naturally wavy hair. In him, as in one who interceded for them with Ka-moo-cum-chux, the Great Spirit, the Modocs had unbounded confidence.

As murmurs grew and spread among the braves, Curly Head Doctor leaped to his feet with his pistol drawn and shouted, "Me-ki-gam-bla-ke-tu! (We will *not* go there!)"

Instantly the rest of the Modocs were on their feet, pistols in their hands, yelling unintelligible threats. Meacham's party, scarcely believing their eyes, drew their guns as one man, prepared to defend themselves to the end, 'though they knew the end meant death.

Slaughter seemed inevitable when Winema sprang between the two lines of belligerent men shouting, "Wait! Wait until I talk! Don't shoot, hear me!" Turning to her aroused people she said, "Mo-lok-a ditch-e ham-konk lok-e sti-nas no-ma gam-bla o-we! (The white Chief talks straight! His heart is good and strong!)"

Back and forth between the lines of armed men, she paced, exhorting first the Modocs and then the white men. To the Indians she said, "If you begin now it will be the end of the Modocs," and to the white men, "Hold your tempers and be patient. There is a misunderstanding. Everything will be all right."

As much by her fearless manner and confident air as by her words, she held them all fairly hypnotized. As she spoke, revolvers, one by one, were slipped back into their holsters. The tenseness of both sides gradually eased.

Captain Jack had taken no part in this demonstration. The crisis over, he grunted as if in disgust and turned to

go, saying, "Ot-we-kau-tux-e! (I am done talking!)"
a signal that the council was ended.

Meacham intercepted him, assuming a brave front
he was far from feeling. "I am your friend," he said.
"I am not afraid of you. Be careful what you do! We
mean peace but we are prepared for war. We will not
begin, but if you do, it shall be the end of your people.
You agreed to go with us. We are ready. Our wagons
will carry your old people and children. We're not
going back without you. You are Chief of the Modocs.
Does a Chief let his men tell him what to do?"

Winema translated the words into Modoc. When
Captain Jack understood, his expressive mouth curved
into a sneer. "I am Chief of the Modocs," he said. "My
men no tell me what to do. White ty-ee, him no tell
Jack what to do. Jack, him do what think best for his
people."

"Then you *will* go with us!" Meacham exclaimed.

"And what if I don't?" The Chief's words were
spoken in a low, but mocking tone.

"Then we'll whip you until you *are* willing!"

"Hmph!" grunted the chief. "I'd be ashamed to
fight so few men with all my braves!"

"These few men are enough to kill *some* Modocs
before they're killed," Meacham asserted boldly. "And
when they're dead more white men will come. I'll give
you until tomorrow to decide. But I warn you, if your
answer is 'no' then you must be prepared to fight! Any
time you want to begin, we'll be ready!"

Captain Jack didn't answer immediately. When he
did, he spoke slowly, grimly. "I will not fire the first
shot. But if you do, the Chief of the Modocs is not
afraid to die!"

CHAPTER III

GOOD-BY TO LOST RIVER

THE quick turn of events left no doubt in the minds of the white men that they were in an extremely precarious position, outnumbered by and at the mercy of an hostile band of Indians. After discussing their course of action, they all agreed that the success of their mission and even the safety of their lives depended upon how convincingly they could keep up a show of bravado.

Their first move was to attempt to get word to the soldiers of their danger. They didn't dare send a messenger out boldly for the purpose, for they knew he would be intercepted and, perhaps, killed by the irate Modocs. Therefore, they waited until dusk when one of their number successfully eluded the guards. Meacham's instructions in the message he carried were that the military squad should approach the Modoc village that night within sound of gunshot, there to await further orders. Under no circumstances were they to charge the camp unless an alarm was given.

Inwardly apprehensive, although outwardly unconcerned and nonchalant Meacham's party watched the darkness close in on the Modoc camp. From the retreat of their improvised shelter, they could see the Indians, mere shadows in the darkness, gathering in the Chief's lodge. Soon the weird chanting of old women and the intonations of the medicine man's voice as he invoked Ka-moo-cum-chux and the spirits of departed warriors, drifted to them on the penetrating breeze from the icy waters of Tule lake.

When these sounds were replaced by the muffled accents of voices, the stranded white men knew that the future welfare of the band, on which hinged their own, was being discussed. It was as well that they could not know the import of Schonchin John's words, strongly supported by Curly Head Doctor, as they argued for massacring Meacham's party that very night. Many of the braves sided with these two, while others upheld Captain Jack and Scarface Charley who were more realistic and sober in their reasoning.

Midnight came and went with the issue still unsettled. Meacham's men anxiously waited by the dim light of their camp fire, the tenseness of their nerves making sleep impossible. Suddenly one of the men sat bolt upright. "Listen!" he whispered hoarsely. "What's that?"

The soft, padding sound made by the moccasined guard as he paced back and forth in front of Meacham's lodge, ceased. In its place came a dull rumble which they soon identified as the pounding of horses' hoofs on the frozen ground. The guard gave the alarm and they could hear him running toward the Chief's lodge.

The confusion of sounds followed in rapid succession . . . shouts of soldiers, rattle of sabres, snapping of sagebrush, the distressed cries of Indians.

Meacham's men grabbed for their guns and ran outside. Everything was in excited turmoil. Indians, terrified by the sudden uproar, came pouring pell-mell from the council lodge, guns in hand, heading straight for the sagebrush. Horses stamped, snorted, plunged; soldiers laughed, shouted and shot into the air. Squaws and children ran here and there, seeking safety.

Captain Knapp saw in a flash what had happened. "Surround the camp!" he shouted to the soldiers. "Quick! Let no one escape! There's not a second to be lost!"

The authoritative command sobered the soldiers, who scattered to carry out his orders. Many of the Indians, not knowing how large a force they had to contend with, thought better of attempting to offer battle. A few of them, like trapped animals, fought for a time, but were quickly subdued. Meacham assured them through Winema that if they remained quiet no one would be harmed.

Several hours remained before daylight would make it possible to take any definite action. In the meantime, Captain Knapp, on investigating the cause of the untimely arrival of the soldiers, learned that since the night was bitterly cold, the men had decided before leaving Linkville, that a little forty-rod whiskey would help warm things up a bit. It had put such "spirit" into their venture that they had forgotten to stop at the right time.

From then on, no one even thought of sleeping. The hours dragged and suspense had become almost unbearable by the time gray dawn began to break over the Lost river country, disclosing about two hundred Indians . . . braves, squaws and children . . . surrounded by a circle of bayonets.

There was no dallying now. The Indians, some sullen, some insolent, were lined up. It was then that Meacham noticed that several of the head men of the tribe were missing, among them Captain Jack, Curly Head Doctor and Schonchin John. A search for them was started immediately. The remainder of the Indians were assured that if they offered no resistance they would be treated fairly, taken to the reservation and given protection, clothing and food.

The attempt to disarm the braves was strenuously resisted. For a few tense moments, anything might have happened, for both red men and white men were armed and defiant. Had the Modoc leaders been present to rally the Indians for a concerted attack, their greater numbers might well have made them the victors.

The white men realized the seriousness of the situation, and taking advantage of the Modoc's disorganization, a few of the soldiers frisked the warriors under the protection of the guns of their comrades. The weapons, once secured, were stacked in a pile and a strong guard placed over them.

Immediate steps were taken for removing the Indians to the reservation. A courier was sent to Fort Klamath for eight wagons in which to pack their goods and supplies and to provide transportation for the women and children. The Indian ponies were rounded up, provisions taken from the caches where they had been stored and everything put in order for the journey.

As these activities progressed without any information of the location of the Chief and his head men, it became more and more certain that they had escaped under cover of darkness. Most of the other Indians were gloomily silent and questioning brought no more than stubborn, noncommittal grunts. But after a vivid

picture had been painted of the punishment the runaways would receive if they did not return willingly,
Meacham was rewarded by having one of the Indian
women tell him she knew their probable hiding place
in the Lava Beds. If she were allowed to go to them,
she said, she felt sure she could induce them to surrender.

The squaw was unusually attractive in spite of
irregular features, and Meacham learned from Winema
that she was Captain Jack's sister, known to the white
men as "Queen Mary" on account of her sagacity and
influence in the tribe. He had heard of her many
times, for she had lived with five or six white men in
the ten years previous, each of whom had been more
than willing to get rid of the squaw when he became
aware of her ability to squander his money.

Realizing that everything was to be gained and
nothing to be lost by sending her on this mission,
Meacham provided a horse for her with instructions to
tell Captain Jack that his people had not been harmed
and that he would be well-treated if he would give
himself up. Otherwise, he would be hunted down mer-
cilessly.

When the wagons which had been sent for arrived,
they were loaded with all kinds of goods that the Indians wished to take with them, including roots and
fish which they had dried for future use. In addition,
the wagons were over-loaded with women, ragged and
unkempt; children, noisy and shamelessly dirty; the
sick and crippled, uncared-for and pitiful.

As the motley wagon procession started to move
across the sagebrush covered valley, the braves rode
alongside on their ponies or plodded behind on foot
with rangy, half-starved dogs tagging at their heels or

taking off in pursuit of real or imaginary jack-rabbits. To the soldiers, who brought up the rear and were stationed alongside the caravan, it seemed that there were at least a half-dozen mongrel canines to every redskin.

The sun was setting over the low hills when they reached Link river. A hasty camp was set up and food prepared for two hundred hungry people. Residents of the little settlement at Linkville, piqued with curiosity by the arrival of the Modoc Indians, gathered around the outskirts of the camp, eager to catch sight of Captain Jack, who was now a notorious character. Keen was their disappointment and renewed was their fear when they learned he had escaped.

In the hope that Queen Mary might be successful in bringing back Captain Jack, Meacham decided to stay for a few days at Link river where supplies were available. At the end of the third day, however, it seemed useless to wait any longer; but no sooner had he given orders to prepare to move on toward Klamath Agency the next morning than Queen Mary appeared.

Captain Jack, Curly Head Doctor, Schonchin John and another brave who had escaped with them, she reported, had agreed to give themselves up if Meacham would promise not to punish them for their escape and would keep the Klamaths from molesting them. The superintendent told Queen Mary to return and assure them that he would comply with their wishes and that they had nothing to fear.

That night, just before time for taps, the four Indians rode into camp. Judging from their expressions and actions, it seemed impossible to determine how they felt about the situation but, at least, they appeared to want to make the best of it. They were greeted warmly by the other Indians, whose resentment had gradually toned down under the kind treatment accorded them. Meacham and his men, also, welcomed the runaways heartily, for their return meant that the purpose for which the white men had risked their lives had been accomplished.

Next morning, the twenty-seventh of December everything was ready for the procession to continue its journey to Klamath Agency. But before starting, Captain Jack approached Meacham with the request that the soldiers be sent on ahead. The armed men frightened the women and children, he claimed, and since none of the Indians now carried weapons, there was no necessity for the presence of the soldiers.

Meacham thought it over carefully before replying. He realized that such a concession was unusual, but he finally decided that to concede to Captain Jack's request would be an expression of confidence in Indian integrity which might be more effective than the protection of the soldiers in insuring the safety of his party. Captain Knapp reluctantly consented and the soldiers galloped off toward Fort Klamath with instructions to round up the Klamaths at a designated spot for a meeting of reconciliation and peace-making with the Modocs.

The morning was bitter cold. The wagon-trail which the caravan followed ran through a mountain pass, blanketed with twenty inches of snow. These obstacles made their progress discouragingly slow. That night they were forced to make camp in the high country, but the next day brought them again to the shore of Klamath lake at the place selected for the meeting with the Klamaths.

The agency Indians had already begun to gather when the strange caravan arrived. Hesitating to mingle

with the Klamaths at first, the Modocs began to set up
their camp in a somewhat protected spot on the long
point which ran out into the lake. The Klamaths chose
a site not far away.

All that day the Klamaths, as well as many of the
Modocs who had previously chosen to remain on the
reservation, continued to arrive. These Modocs and
members of Captain Jack's returning band were quick
to renew old friendships, exchanging banter and stories
of experiences during the five years of their separation.

Probably much of the time of waiting would have
been spent in gambling, according to the Indian custom, if Captain Jack had not requested Meacham to
issue an order against it. Jack knew from long experience what inveterate gamblers the Indians were, and
what confusion of property would result if something
were not done to curb it. Even domestic relations had a
way of being upset, for in the heat of the game the
braves often staked their wives and daughters on the
throw of a stick.

Next morning preparations were complete for the
peace making. A large pine tree standing between the
Modoc and the Klamath camps was used as a point
though which a line was drawn. Each tribe assembled
on its own side of the line under the tree's wide-spread-
ing branches; the Klamaths bold and self-confident,
even a little condescending. The Modocs, on the other
hand, assembled reluctantly, stolid for the most part.
but unable to conceal their chagrin completely.

When everything was ready for the beginning of the
"peace talk", Meacham took his position at the base of
the stately pine tree, and addressed the Indians with
the help of an interpreter. "You meet to-day in peace to
bury all the bad past," he said. "You are of the same

blood, the same heart. You are to live as neighbors. This country belongs to you all alike. Your interests are one. You must shake hands and be friends."

Then he called the Chiefs of the two tribes forward. Allen David, Chief of the Klamaths, stepped unhesitatingly up to his side of the line; a tall, impressive Indian with features fine and intelligent, although deeply lined with age. Captain Jack came forward more diffidently. Only a few feet apart, the two warrior chieftains, ancient enemies, stood gazing into each other's eyes, neither speaking a word.

Meacham gave a twig of pine to each Chief, and laid a hatchet on the ground between them. Advancing, each Chief knelt and placed his pine bough over the axe as a symbol that they had buried the hatchet and become friends. As they arose, each one placed his foot upon it, and they grasped hands, looking long into each other's eyes, yet without a spoken word.

Then they stepped back and the subchiefs of each tribe came forward, and followed the example of their chieftains until all had pledged themselves to peace and friendship.

When the ceremony was over, Allen David stepped forward and fixed his gaze intently upon Captain Jack. He was fully six feet in height, straight and powerfully proportioned. In measured sentences, his voice clear and vibrant, he spoke:

"I see you. I see your eyes. Your skin is red like my own. I will show you my heart. We have long been enemies. Many of our brave muck-a-lux (people) are dead. The ground is red with their blood.

"Their bones have been carried by the coyotes to the mountains and scattered among the rocks. Our people are melting away like snow. We see the White Chief is strong. The law is strong. We cannot be Indians any longer. We must take the white man's law. The law of our fathers is dead.

"The White Chief brought you here. We have made friends. We have washed each other's hands. They are not bloody, now. We have buried all the bad blood. We will not dig it up again. The white man sees us. Soch-e-la Ka-moo-cum-chux. The Great Spirit is looking at our hearts. The sun is witness between us. The mountains are looking at us."

Turning to the tall tree beneath which he stood, he made a gesture of great dignity and continued: "This pine tree is a witness, Oh my people! When you see this tree remember that it is a witness that here we made friends with the Moadocus. Never cut down that tree. Let the arm be broken that would hurt it. Let the hand die that would break a twig from it. So long as snow shall fall on Yainax mountain, let it stand. Long as the white rabbit shall run in the manzanita groves, let it stand. Let our children play around it. Let the young people dance under its branches. Let the old men smoke together in its shade. Let this tree stand forever as a witness. I have spoken."

Captain Jack, trying to conceal how deeply he was affected by this speech, made his reply, his eyes steadfast upon Allen David. In a softly modulated voice characteristic of him, he began hesitatingly: "The White Chief brought me here. I felt ashamed for my people because they were poor. I felt like a man in a strange country without a father. My heart was afraid. I have heard your words. They warm my heart. I am not strange now. We are enemies no longer. The blood is all washed from our hands. We have buried the past. We have forgotten that we were enemies. We will not throw away the White Chief's words. We will not hide them in the grass.

"I have planted a strong stake in the ground. I have tied myself with a strong rope. I will not pull up the stake. I will not break the rope. My heart is the heart of my people. I am their words. I am not speaking for myself. I speak their hearts. My heart comes up into my mouth. I cannot keep it down with a sharp stick. I have spoken."

Meacham stepped forward and spoke of his assurance that their troubles were at an end, and commended them on the fine spirit they had shown. They would meet again in the afternoon, he told them, to receive the annuity goods issued by the government in conformity with the treaty of 1864. Thus the "peace talk" came to an end.

The Indians scattered, Klamaths and Modocs mingling freely, apparently happy over the reconciliation which had taken place. Ma-mak-sti-nas (friendships) were renewed and the Modocs in particular eagerly awaited the afternoon meeting. They had received goods only once before, having forfeited their rights to them for four years by remaining away from the reservation. During that time their clothing and blankets had dwindled, and now they looked forward to receiving new ones as happily as children awaiting the coming of Santa Claus.

When preparations were completed, Meacham summoned them together once more. Each tribe formed in a large semi-circle with the Chief and head men seated in the center, the squaws and children seated in rows behind them. When they were all in their places, the distribution was begun.

First, the blankets were distributed. Two of these

were given to each Chief and each subchief, and one apiece to each of the other Indians, except the very small children, each of whom received half a blanket. The clothing consisted of a woolen shirt and enough cloth for one pair of trousers for each man; yards of flannel dress goods and a pattern for each woman and each child. Thread, needles and buttons were generously distributed.

When the Indians had received their respective shares, they proudly carried the new possessions to their camps, located along the lake shore. As they left the assembly, they presented a picturesque and incongruous scene, for it must be remembered that they did not go with feathered head dresses streaming in the wind and blankets around their shoulders. Already they had substituted many of the ways of white men for their native customs which resulted in an odd combination of old and new.

The shelters to which the Indians returned were equally heterogeneous, being constructed of all sorts of materials. Some were ordinary canvas tents obtained from the government, but most of them were made of a framework of willow poles, covered with wagon sheets, blankets, tule matting or anything else easily obtainable.

The squaws, having little regard for order, and not knowing how to take proper care of things, temporarily spread out the new dress-goods for bedding or stuffed it into baskets or sacks with no thought of wrinkles or dirt. Later they would laboriously make them up into crude clothing.

To the white men, who looked on as the Indians went about their daily routine, there seemed to be neither rhyme nor reason to their habits of eating and sleeping. They apparently had no regular hours for meals, each one suiting his own appetite. Their sleep was equally irregular. They went to bed when they were tired and got up when they were rested, each following his own fancy.

One of the government's oxen had been slaughtered the day before and distributed among the Indians for food. Strange as it seemed to the white men, even the "head and pluck", which meant everything but the dressed meat, were in great demand. These were considered a great delicacy by the Indians, who cooked them over a fire made in a hole, dug in the ground, in which the coals were allowed to collect. They dropped the "head and pluck" of the ox into the hole, hair, horns and all. Coals were shovelled in on top, then a layer of dirt. The fire was rebuilt over the spot and several hours allowed for the "head and pluck" to cook.

In due time, it was dug out and attacked with knives by the hungry Indians who proceeded to carve and eat. If some of the meat turned out to be too rare, it was tossed back on the coals and allowed to char. This process was repeated until every scrap was gone, even the bones.

The camp activities quieted down as dusk began to settle over the encampment. Indian ponies grazed contentedly on the winter grass covering the flat land across which high mountains on the opposite shore of the lake cast their shadows. The sun slowly slipped to rest over a sharp-pointed peak, seeming to split the crown in two, then suddenly dropped from sight. The Indian boys and girls recalled the story of how the sun-god burned a hole in the top of the mountain and buried himself there.

A chill crept over everything with the setting of the

sun while the shadows continued their climb up the steep slopes behind the camp. In the half-light, the teamsters heaped up a great pile of pitch-logs in preparation for the "cultus wa-wa" (big free talk) which had been planned for the evening.

Soon new shadows leapt into life as crackling flames licked up the darkness. Out of these shadows, men began to gather: long-haired yet beardless Indians and short-haired, bearded white men. There was constant shifting among them as the smoke compelled first one, then another, to take a different position from one side of the fire to the other. A self-conscious silence prevailed as men who had formerly been enemies gathered around their first peace-council fire.

When everything was ready, a white man arose and in simple words tried to explain to these natives of a different race the meaning of new laws, new religion and new habits which were to be theirs. The red men listened thoughtfully.When the opportunity was given, an old Indian stood up, his superstitions and beliefs clinging to him like a worn out blanket in tatters. He seemed to be grasping the old ideas with one hand and reaching out with the other for the new ones.

He spoke with dignity of Ka-moo-cum-chux, the Great Spirit, in whom his fathers had believed, apologizing at the same time for the ignorance of himself and his people. This Indian was Link River Joe, and he still remembered some of the impressions he had received on visiting The Dalles Methodist mission twenty years before.

The interpreter reported him as saying, "I have long heard of the white man's religion. I have heard how the Holy Spirit comes to him. I wonder if it will ever come to my people. I am old. I cannot live long. Maybe, it has come now. I feel like a new kind of fire is in my heart. Maybe, you have brought this Holy Spirit.

"I think you have. When you came here first, we were all in bad blood. Now I see Klamaths, Modocs and Yahooskin Snakes all around me, like brothers. No common man could do this. Maybe you are a holy spirit."

This led to a discussion of religion and other subjects until someone happened to remark, "To-morrow will be New Year's day." Immediately the Indians, eager and curious, wanted to know how they could tell when the New Year's day would come. Meacham held up his watch and said, "When all the little sticks on the face of this watch are in a straight line, the old year will die in the West and a new one will be born in the East."

Allen David asked that the watch be passed around so everyone could see, and that a pistol be fired at the exact moment. The white men were far from adverse to a little celebration, so Meacham consented after being assured that the shot would cause no alarm.

Just before twelve o'clock, Meacham held the pistol above his head and announced, "In three minutes 1869 will be dead. Two minutes now . . . now but one." The stillness was painful. "A half minute more . . . " Five hundred redmen held their breath, awaiting the signal; every eye rested on the pistol trigger.

The gun blazed away, making the hills and lake reverberate with the report, as hundreds of voices rose in a chant of farewell to 1869. Then turning from the West to the East, they sent up a rousing hail of welcome to 1870.

CHAPTER IV

BAD BLOOD

THE Modocs greeted the new year with mixed hope and misgiving. No matter how bright the prospects of life were on the Klamath reservation, no matter how attractive the annuity goods which were now their right, they could not escape the feeling of homesickness for their old Lost river country.

The broad, frozen expanse of Upper Klamath lake, stretching some forty miles in length and ten to fifteen miles in width, seemed cheerless and unfriendly in comparison to the lazy winding of their Lost river. And although their camp at Modoc Point afforded ideal fishing, grazing for their horses and timber for their houses, they still preferred the smell of their accustomed sagebrush and juniper to that of the pines.

Nevertheless, the Modocs accepted the situation with good grace and in a few days were comfortably settled. They began to think of their camp in terms of permanency and this, abetted by the threat of winter's hardships on account of cold, spurred them to set about immediate plans for making log houses like the white men and the Klamaths had.

Tools and equipment were essential to carrying out this project, so Captain Jack and a few of his head men one day mounted their ponies and rode fifteen miles or so to Klamath Agency, headquarters for the reservation, and presented themselves before Captain Knapp, the Indian agent. To him they outlined their plans and asked for his cooperation.

Now that the Modocs had been rounded up and Meacham had returned to his headquarters at Salem, Captain Knapp's primary interests had turned elsewhere and the less bother the renegade band was the better he liked it. His reply, therefore, was sadly lacking in the encouragement and personal interest which would have meant so much to the Modocs in getting adjusted to their new home. His consent to their request was given condescendingly and more to get rid of them quickly than because he fully approved, for his words and tone of voice implied that he had little faith in their ability to use the tools to advantage, once they had them.

But in spite of this indifference, Captain Jack and his men were happy, indeed, when they rode into camp that night well provided with chopping axes, cross-cut saws, wedges, maul rings and other tools necessary to the task of building homes. They realized it was no mean job they had set for themselves, for the lumber they must use was still standing timber, and they were inexperienced in the use of the strange tools they had acquired.

Next morning every able bodied man in the band was ready to start the race with the chill winds and snows of winter, the worst of which still lay ahead. Like beavers they set about falling trees, splitting them into rails and piling them up, ready to be hauled to the camp. In a few days, so wholehearted was their labor, they had enough of the timber cut so that some of the men could begin putting together the first house . . . the house that was to belong to their Chief, Captain Jack.

Great was their disappointment when a snow storm swept down from the mountains during the night to halt their work. For a day or so they were forced to be idle and huddle about their fires for protection against the bitter north wind and swirling whiteness, but as soon as the sun shone once more, they eagerly resumed their work.

A group of them started early that morning for the wooded slope where they had piled the rails a short distance from their camp. Arriving there, consternation replaced the good spirits with which they had started out. The snow was packed down by the tramping of many feet, the marks of wagon wheels were plainly visible in the snow . . . and about half of their rails were nowhere to be found!

One of the men raced back to camp, breathlessly telling Captain Jack what they had seen. The Chief listened and said nothing, but silently accompanied the messenger back to the woods. After noting in detail the marks left around the pile of rails, he turned to his men with the one word, "Klamaths". Alone he followed the wagon trail a short distance through the woods, then returned and ordered the men to go on with their work.

This they did, although most of them would have preferred to track down the thieves, who had stolen the rails, and demand the return of them on the threat of death. That day they worked unmolested, but when they returned earlier than usual next morning, they surprised five or six Klamaths who were loading rails into a wagon. The thieves did not stop on seeing the Modocs, but kept right on loading, with an insolence that, to the hot-tempered Modocs, was unbearable.

Muttering threats, the Modocs started across the clearing, wielding their axes threateningly. But a curt command from Captain Jack stopped them in their tracks.

"Klamaths only try to pick fight," Captain Jack told his men. "Must not quarrel with Klamaths. Modocs sure to get blame." Solemnly he laid his gun on the ground. Ordering his comrades to stay where they were, he approached the intruders alone and demanded of the nearest Klamath by what authority they were hauling off rails which belonged to the Modocs.

"By my authority!" the Klamath boasted, striking himself on the chest. "It is our timber. You can use our timber but it belongs to us. You can make rails but you must give us some of them. They are really all ours. But we will let you keep some."

Other Klamath Indians crowded around Captain Jack and took turn about taunting him, calling the Modocs "hal-lo-e-me till-i-cum" (strangers) and insisting they had no business on Klamath land. One old Klamath brave went so far as to say, "I am a Klamath. I have always lived on this land. It is my land. This is not your country. The Lost river country is where you belong. If you cut rails from my timber, I will take them. The mighty Captain Jack will have to pay tribute to me or go back to his Lost river country!"

During all of these insults, Captain Jack said nothing. But when they ran out of taunts, he faced them unflinchingly. "I am a Modoc," he said, never raising his voice above his ordinary tone but biting his words short.

"I am Chief of the Modocs. I am not afraid of you, but I will not quarrel with you. I made a promise under great peace-tree and I will keep my promise. Your memories are short. You have already forgotten the agreement made at the peace-tree. I will see Agent Knapp. He will see that you keep the peace-tree agreement. He will see that you are punished."

With that Captain Jack turned on his heel and strode back to where his men were waiting. He told them what the Klamaths had said, adding that he felt sure their Chief, Allen David, knew nothing of what was going on. He ordered them to quit work and return to the camp, until he could ride to Klamath Agency and place the matter before Agent Knapp.

Captain Jack chose Bogus Charley, a tall, arrow-straight young brave, who could "talk white man's talk" better than any one else in the tribe, to go with him. The two mounted their ponies and by noon they reached the reservation headquarters. There they encountered a group of Klamaths who made them the butt of taunts and jeers; accused them of being everything from horse thieves to cowards.

Captain Jack tried to ignore the bantering Klamaths, but they pushed in on the two men, effectively blocking their path. Bogus Charley, more quick-tempered than his Chief, swung his lithe, powerful body from his pony to the ground and challenged in a stentorian voice any man among them to call him a coward to his face.

Anything might have happened in the next few minutes had not Captain Knapp heard the rumpus going on outside and stepped to the door of his office at that moment. At a word from him, the Klamaths quieted and fell back.

The agent was not pleased to see who his visitors

were and he ushered them into his office brusquely, asking what he could do for them. Bogus Charley did the talking, his quick darting eyes still ablaze, his voice still booming. He told how the Klamaths had stolen their rails and tried to pick a quarrel with them by claiming the Modocs had no right on the reservation. "We have come to ask you to put a stop to all this," he finished.

Knapp went on with some work he had at his desk for a few moments before he replied, while the two Indians shifted uneasily from one foot to another. Then, as if disposing of a petty annoyance, he suggested that Captain Jack move his people to a site nearer the agency on Williamson river. "Just let your rails go and move as soon as you can," he said bluntly. "Then if the Klamaths bother you there, I will attend to them." He turned back to his papers as if to close the interview but as the two Indians started to leave the office, he looked up quickly and added, "But whatever you do, don't fight with them. Leave everything to me."

Bogus Charley merely grunted and the two men were soon on their ponies bound for camp. They were far from satisfied with the "protection" offered by the agent, for it meant the loss of the work they had already done as well as the time it would take to move camp— a difficult task at that time of year.

By the time Captain Jack's band was settled on Williamson river, some five miles from their former location, it seemed useless to attempt any more work, for winter was now doing its worst, piling snow several feet deep in the woods before winds blowing with fury. They could only make the best of it and wait for spring. During this time the Modocs got along tolerably well with the Klamaths, for they now had nothing their an-

Scarface Charley, head man under Captain Jack

(Photo by Signal Corps, U. S. Army)

Winema

tagonists might covet, and, indeed, the weather prevented the two tribes from seeing much of each other.

In March, after a trip to their traditional fishing grounds, the Modocs once more began the work of building permanent homes for themselves. They had finished hewing out two or three hundred rails and had begun to think that the Klamaths would leave them alone, but the trouble-makers returned. The Klamaths had become more bold after having accomplished their previous exploit with impunity and were more insolent and overbearing than before, carrying off more rails belonging to the Modocs.

Still Captain Jack refused to make a violent issue of it. Once more he appeared before Captain Knapp. This time he was told to go on with his work, that the agent would "make it all right".

In the press of other business, however, Knapp did nothing about it and the Klamaths continued their pilfering and heckling more boldly than ever. Captain Jack tried to remonstrate with them and remind them of the peace making and the rights conceded to the Modocs, but it did no good.

The Klamaths jeered at him for being so poor that he and his people had to live off the Klamaths. Very patronizingly they would say, "You can stay here, yes; but it is our country. You can catch fish, but they are our fish." Whereupon, they would make off with more rails.

A third time Captain Jack went to Agent Knapp. Angry and irritated at being so persistently annoyed with Captain Jack's troubles, Knapp pointedly told the Modoc Chief, "Look here! If you come to me again I'm going to put you where you'll never be bothered by the Klamaths or anyone else. I'll move you once more

and this time you'll stay moved. I'll leave it up to you
to find a place where you won't always be stepping on
the Klamath's toes."

Captain Jack and his braves left Knapp's office that
day with their faith in government promises, the agent's
protection and the value of treaties completely shattered. Half-heartedly they rode about the country
looking for a possible camp site, but everywhere there
seemed to be Klamaths to claim prior rights. They
returned to camp that night greatly discouraged, and
with a new plan formulating in their minds. The Chief
called his people together around the council fire and
told them just how things stood.

"Already I have talked with Knapp three times," he
said. "Knapp has no heart for us. I am afraid he is not a
good man. He does not keep the superintendent's
promises. Who wants to stay with a man who has no
heart for us? Let us leave this place and go back to our
Lost river home."

The idea was not new to many of the Modocs, who
had been impatient with Captain Jack's stubborn determination to stand by the peace agreement if it were
at all possible. Unknown to him, several of the braves
had been agitating for some time in favor of the action
he now suggested and they were for making the move
at once.

Others, of a more conservative nature and those more
inclined to take the path of easiest resistance even at a
sacrifice to their pride, argued heatedly in favor of remaining, especially since to leave would mean relin-
quishing the supplies of food, clothing and blankets
which were their lot as wards of the government.

Far into the night the discussion went on. The Indians were torn between the desire for goods and the

indignation at the way they had been treated both by the Klamaths and by the agent whose protection they had claimed as their right. A few years before, the matter would have been settled once and for all by the decision of the Chief, but having learned the white men's ways, the Chief no longer had absolute authority. Thus the question was put to a vote and the proposition to return to their sagebrush country carried by a large majority.

One thing they had not learned, however, and that was that the minority should abide by the decision of the majority. Those who had opposed the plan refused to go, so the band was split, a few Indians sitting stolidly and watching the hasty preparations of others who did not even wait until morning to pack their belongings and round up their horses.

By the time the sun began to tint the gray waters of Klamath lake, fifty Modoc braves and their families had turned their backs on the Klamath reservation, the place of disappointed hopes, and were traveling with their faces to the south where they knew their rights on Lost river would not be disputed . . . at least by the Klamaths.

When it was discovered that they had gone, Captain Knapp must have considered it good riddance, for he made no immediate effort to force them back. Instead he rounded up the few who had remained, foremost among whom was old Chief Schonchin, and placed them under the supervision of Oliver Applegate, sub-agent at Yainax on the eastern section of the reservation far from the scene of their former troubles.

As one moon followed another, many of the renegade Chief's warriors renewed their former acquaintances in the little mining center of Yreka. Here they found a sympathetic hearing for their troubles among the lower class men of the town with whom they swapped Pit river squaws they had captured, for goods and trinkets they desired.

Captain Jack, too, often went to Yreka where he succeeded in gaining the attention and interest of a few of the leading citizens. From them he received letters of commendation which strengthened in him the feeling that he had been justified in leaving the reservation. Naturally, the support of these men made him more determined to resist any efforts to force his people to go back to the reservation.

Such attempts were negligible at first, but the Modocs had not been re-established long in the Lost river country until the people who had settled there, began to agitate for their removal. At last unfriendly feeling reached such a high pitch that the government officials were forced to take notice of it. As one negotiation after another failed, it became apparent that conditions were so bad that only a show of military power could change them.

At this critical time circumstances framed a charge of "murder" against Captain Jack, the consequences of which threw every man, woman and child in the valley into a state of alarm. The "murder" charge grew out of the illness of one of the Modoc children for whom, in the absence of Curly Head Doctor, Captain Jack had employed an Indian medicine man from another tribe, paying the fee in advance. According to Indian custom, this procedure guaranteed that the child would recover. In the event that the child died, the life of the medicine man was at the mercy of the friends of the deceased. The child did die, whereupon Captain Jack exercised his ancient prerogative and saw to it that the doctor joined his patient in short order.

He was acting in accordance with the traditions of his people, but the white man's law had superseded those traditions. What had been an approved tribal usage had suddenly become a crime of the first degree.

The friends of the murdered man appealed to the white man's law, and an effort was made to arrest Captain Jack. His escape and defiance of the government, for attempting to punish him by a law that was not his law, caused terror to run rampant among the settlers Many of them sent their families over the mountains by stage-coach and wagon to the Rogue river settlement to remain until their safety at home was assured. Men went about their work armed with revolvers for instant action, their rifles always close at hand. As long as Captain Jack was at large, infuriated, as he was, by the ill-treatment with which he thought the government had served him, the residents of the valley knew they would have no peace. They waited, fearful and anxious, for news of what was to be done to get rid of this man whom they had come to consider a desperado of the worst kind.

When the news did come, these sturdy frontiersmen, men of action, fumed and fretted in their impatience and disapproval. Those who had the power to set forces in motion that would humble these renegade Modocs were still convinced that a reconciliation could be effected without bloodshed.

Meacham, who was still in office as Superintendent of Indian Affairs, requested of General Edward R. S. Canby, commander of the Department of the Columbia, that military action be delayed until one more effort had been made to settle things peaceably, and pending this, that the order for Captain Jack's arrest be revoked. With considerable misgiving, Canby consented and issued the necessary orders.

The responsibility for making the attempt to bring Captain Jack to terms was placed in the hands of Colonel E. Otis and Major J. N. High. These two army officers, pompous and resplendent in their military trappings, met in Linkville and decided to try to communicate with the renegade Chief through his sister, Queen Mary.

She agreed to do what she could and that night, soon after dark, she rode off on horseback in quest of her brother, promising to bring back his reply the next morning. She returned with word that Captain Jack would agree to meet the peace men if they were not armed and if white men and Indians should each have the same number of men. Further communications followed with Queen Mary acting as go-between until arrangements in conformity with the Chief's conditions were complete.

The place set for the meeting was in a wild, desolate part of the country, called Lost River Gap, about twelve miles from Linkville. At the time appointed, Colonel Otis, Major High, Ivan Applegate, Oliver Applegate and Dave Hill, a trusted Klamath scout, gathered at a one-room, abandoned shack, the only shelter the place afforded. There was not a sign of a Modoc.

Anxiously they kept scanning the nearby hills, as the time for the meeting came and went. At last, after over two nerve-wracking hours of waiting, one of them made out a file of Indians on horseback, following the course of Lost river toward the gap.

Clumps of juniper trees and large lava boulders

partly concealed them from view, but long before they arrived, they realized that every member of Captain Jack's band was there, outnumbering their own party at least seven to one. The Indians left their horses in a clump of juniper trees with guards to watch them and stacked their rifles against a large boulder, much to the relief of the men watching from across the river.

Crossing the stream single file on a log, they approached without relaxing their stolid faces into anything that might be interpreted as a friendly greeting. Gruffly they elbowed their way into the little room where the council was to be held.

Fearing their intention, Oliver Applegate, tall and impressive, moved about among the group. By rubbing against them, he could feel the butts of revolvers secreted beneath their clothing and thus discovered that nearly all of them were armed. As it happened, the commission, fearing to go completely unarmed, also had concealed revolvers. The guns carried by these redskins, they knew, were practically as good as their own, most of them having been stolen from the settlers or traded for horses.

In a room packed with hostile Indians, with only one door for an exit, the efforts toward reconciliation began. Colonel Otis stood behind a rickety table at which Oliver Applegate, one of the few white men who could speak and understand the Modoc jargon, sat taking careful notes of the proceedings. First of all, Captain Jack was asked to state his grievances.

He pushed forward among his tribesmen who were leaning against the walls, standing about or squatting on the floor. With Applegate as interpreter, Captain Jack told of the way the Klamaths had treated them on the reservation and he blamed the government for failing to protect his people according to Meacham's promise made at the peace-making. He insisted that since the government had not kept its promise, he didn't have to keep his. As for the crime of murder with which he was charged, he argued that killing the medicine man was not a crime under Indian law. Why should he be judged by a law that was not his law?

The crux of it all was, Jack declared, that the Modocs and Klamaths could never live together in peace. Having tried it twice, he and his band were determined to stay where they belonged in their Lost river country.

Colonel Otis assured him of protection and the choice of any location on the Klamath reservation that was unoccupied. To this, as to all other offers, Captain Jack remained stubbornly opposed. He refused even to consider them, referring to former broken promises.

At this Colonel Otis' anger and irritation exploded volubly. Wrenching around his cartridge belt to bring his revolver within easy reach, he unwittingly brought it into full view. As inconspicuously as possible all the other peace commissioners did the same thing, while the Indians could be seen stealthily shifting their hands nearer their guns.

Scarface Charley quickly took in these maneuvers. Turning to Major High he asked what they were going to do. High replied, "There's no use trying to hide it any longer. We know you came here to kill us. But if you do it, some of you are going to die first and you'll be the first one!"

Captain Jack stepped between them. He whispered something to Scarface Charley, turning abruptly, motioning for Scarface and Major High to follow him. Out through the door they went, the others making

way for them grudgingly. It looked like the finish of
Major High.

Once outside, Captain Jack walked some distance
from the cabin and squatted down in the shade of a
juniper tree. Scarface and Major High sat down beside
him. For what seemed an eternity to Major High, not
a word was uttered as each man waited for the other
one to begin.

At last Captain Jack jabbed a sharp stick that he held
into the ground and fixed upon Major High his black,
piercing eyes. He spoke softly, but even before Scarface's interpretation, Major High felt the bite in his
words. "We no want to kill you white men," he said.
"We no want your dead bodies. They no good to us.
We want our Lost river country. You no give it to us,
we will kill you then. We no 'fraid to die. We die
rather than give up what belongs to us. Lost river belong to our people always. We cannot live with Klamaths. Must be stone wall from earth to sky between us.
We only want to be left alone. We tired of talk, talk,
all time talk!"

Major High tried to explain through the aid of
Scarface that Captain Jack was taking the wrong course;
that if his braves killed Otis and his men the army
would send all its soldiers and they would never rest
until they had killed every Modoc. Moreover, High
played his last card . . . the one that had been held out
until it was certain every other means would fail.

"The Great White Father wants to play fair with
your people," High said. "But some of the men he has
trusted to do that have made a mistake. The white
men are not enemies of the Modocs unless you make
them so. Here's what we'll do. If you will agree to
prevent your people from molesting the white settlers

until arrangements are completed, we'll try to secure a small reservation for you at the mouth of Lost river."

Captain Jack made no reply for some time. At last he rose to his feet. "Good," he said. "If you will do that, we no kill you now. You tell your men, I tell my men. They all right. I tell my braves not to kill white men 'til I say. We go in."

Inside once more, Major High explained to the others what had transpired, and a small, rude map was made, showing the location of the proposed reservation. Captain Jack was given to understand that it might be some time before a decision could be made at Washington, and that, in the meantime, he must keep his people under control.

The Indians filed out of the cabin, crossed the river where they mounted their ponies and rode west into the sunset. In the cabin, five men, who had just escaped death at the hands of these same Indians, once more breathed freely and prepared to do their best to avert hostilities for all time.

CHAPTER V

RED-HANDED REVENGE

THE matter of providing a small reservation on Lost river for the Modocs was immediately placed before the authorities at Washington, D. C. There it met with conflicting opinions, red tape and under-estimation of the seriousness of the situation with the result that month after month passed with no decision. Lacking higher authority, the local representatives were powerless to act.

Thus the machinery for putting into effect the promise made to the Modocs was practically at a standstill for two years. But not so the activities of the Indians! They grew restless and impatient, lost faith in the peace negotiations, and a certain faction of the band, unsanctioned by their Chief, took vengeance on the white men of the valley. They stole horses, demanded hay for their animals and food for themselves; threatened women in the absence of their husbands, until the word "Modoc" became a cause for terror.

As conditions grew worse, the patience of the settlers, at last, reached its limits. There must be a show-down with Captain Jack and without delay. Why should a band of renegade Indians terrorize the citizens of a strong government when there were soldiers within reach?

In the little settlement of Linkville excitement ran high. The stockmen and ranchers gathered there, threatened to take things into their own hands if the soldiers were afraid of Captain Jack. They would organize a company of volunteers and drive those Modocs back on the reservation. There would be no trifling with *them* once they got started.

Into such an atmosphere, T. B. Odeneal, who had only recently succeeded A. B. Meacham as Superintendent of Indian Affairs for Oregon, was injected when he rode into Linkville late in November, with instructions to settle the Modoc trouble permanently, if possible. Before he had time to catch the feverishness of the citizens, he sent a courier to contact Captain Jack. The message requested the Modoc Chief to meet Odeneal at Linkville for a conference.

The renegade Chief refused. He had no illusions about the hatred the white men of the Klamath country now held for him. He knew that to meet Odeneal at Linkville would be the equivalent of giving up his life.

Odeneal compromised by agreeing to meet Jack at Lost river two days later. In the meantime, the superintendent began to show symptoms indicating that the germ of the prevalent "Indian fever" had begun its work on him. One of the first signs exhibited itself when, instead of preparing for the peace conference with the Indian Chief, he sent Ivan Applegate to Fort Klamath with a request for fifty soldiers to bring in the renegades.

This hasty action under the influence of the panicky

demands of the citizens was contrary to all the well-seasoned advice of those who really knew the situation. General Canby, Commander of the Department of the Columbia, had sent orders to make the removal "peaceably if you can, forcibly if you must, but if troops are issued, enough men should be sent to place the result beyond peradventure."

Oliver Applegate's advice was the same. Applegate, although not yet thirty, had under his supervision nearly five hundred Modoc, Klamath and Snake Indians at Yainax station. He realized the danger, for he had grown up on the frontier and knew the Modocs. He also recognized that if hostilities broke out with the renegade band, there would very likely be an uprising of the Indians already on the reservation. He had urgently recommended that no action oe taken to bring in Captain Jack until at least one hundred and fifty soldiers had been stationed in the Klamath country.

Colonel John Green, in command of the troops at Fort Klamath, also yielded to pressure from the settlers. It happened that he couldn't spare the fifty soldiers requested, so he dispatched thirty-five under a seasoned officer, Captain Jackson. When Green was reminded of Canby's orders, he replied, "But if I don't send the troops they'll all think we're afraid of those redskins!" These troopers from Fort Klamath reached Linkville on horseback November 28, 1872.

Late in the evening of the same day, Oliver Applegate, who had been asked to come in from Yainax to go with the party to make terms with Captain Jack, dismounted before the Linkville hotel. There the young subagent, very prepossessing in appearance and bearing, met Odeneal. On learning of the change in plans, Applegate made no secret of his disapproval, at which the new superintendent became somewhat apologetic at having to admit that he had given little thought to the possibility of a peaceful settlement. The orders, he repeated with emphasis on the last phrase, were to make the removal "peaceably if you can, forcibly if you must". "Nobody around here thinks that we can talk them into coming back, but of course we'll give them a chance to come in voluntarily before we make an attack," Odeneal conceded.

While they were talking, Applegate saw two men mount their horses and gallop away, one of them wearing a black cape which streamed behind him in the breeze. "Who're those fellows?" he inquired.

"That's One-Arm Brown, messenger for the Indian service who came down from Salem with me, and Dennis Crawley, a rancher who lives near Captain Jack's camp," Odeneal informed him. "I've sent them ahead to warn the settlers that hostilities are imminent."

Further conversation between Odeneal and Applegate was cut short by a group of soldiers who approached them, laughing and joking as they made light of the prospective "Injun party". Applegate turned away in disgust, and went off to sound out the general attitude of the townspeople.

He found five or six men who volunteered to go along to "see the fireworks" and help bring in the Modocs should they consent to come peaceably. Applegate said it was agreeable to him, and obtained Odeneal's consent for these "volunteers" to accompany the soldiers.

About midnight the troopers were lined up and given their instructions, for it was planned that they should be at the Modoc camp by daybreak. Driving sleet had begun to pelt down on the men, whose lightheartedness gave way to the depressing influence of an ominously black and disagreeable night. As they rode toward the Indian village, their discomfort increased for the sleet gave way to biting wind that froze their clothing as stiff as plaster casts.

At the Lone Pine ford on Lost river, Captain Jackson called a halt. They were about seven miles from Captain Jack's camp now, and it was four o'clock in the morning. The Modocs, they knew, were encamped on both sides of the river. Their Chief, and the major portion of the band, were on the west bank, while one of the subchiefs, Hooker Jim, and about fourteen braves were camped on the east side.

Accordingly, the party divided there. Applegate and the five volunteers received orders from Captain Jackson to cross the ford to the east side of the river and go to Crawley's cabin, which overlooked both camps from its location on a small knoll. They were ordered to hold it as a rallying point at all costs and under no conditions to make an offensive attack.

Captain Jackson's party was to approach the Modoc village from the west. With this understanding, the horses' hoofs once more crunched noisily over the frozen ground as the two parties advanced on the Modocs.

The troops left the road to lessen the chances of detection by the wily redskins, and found it hard going through the thick sagebrush in the darkness. By daylight, they were still about a mile from their goal, but they continued to push forward.

Meanwhile Applegate's men had taken position in a gulch about seventy-five yards from the Crawley cabin on the east side of the river where One-Arm Brown and Crawley joined them. They had learned, they said, that some one had warned the settlers, saving them the trouble of doing so.

Cramped and numb with cold, they waited for what seemed an eternity before they saw Captain Jackson's men approach the camp, dismount and line up before the Chief's lodge in the village. Almost immediately Captain Jack, and a few of his braves appeared, startled from their sleep by this sudden invasion.

Captain Jackson quietly ordered them to lay down their guns while they had a talk. Every Indian looked to see whether their Chief would obey the order before they complied. "Your soldier mans all armed" Captain Jack said. "What for you want us to give up guns? What for you wake my people out of sleep just for talk? Superintendent, him say he come before send soldiers. What for he no do like he say?"

Captain Jackson explained through Ivan Applegate, who had accompanied the troops as guide and interpreter, that they didn't want to harm the Modocs. "We brought the soldiers to take you safely back to the reservation where a fine place has been prepared for you at Yainax," he said. "If you lay down your guns and go peaceably, the soldiers will be your friends. If not they will have to be your enemies and force you to go. You can make your own choice, but go you must." Captain Jack hesitated an instant, then reluctantly laid down his gun, and the other Indians followed his example.

Among the civilians watching from the east bank, the tension of waiting had reached a point where One-Arm Brown could stand it no longer. He jumped up and asked Applegate's permission to see what was happening in the other camp; but without waiting for a reply, he leapt on his horse and went galloping down the hill toward the river before anyone could stop him. All his comrades could see was the black cape he habitually wore to conceal the stub of his arm, billowing behind him.

They watched anxiously as he exchanged a few words with Ivan Applegate, who had come down to the opposite bank of the river. In a few minutes he came galloping back. "It's all right," he shouted, jumping the gulch without stopping. "Everything's settled! They're going peaceably. Come on let's round up the redskins on this side!" Away he rode, straight for Hooker Jim's camp.

Before Applegate's eyes flashed a mental picture of just what would happen when One-Arm Brown came face to face with Hooker Jim, a tall, powerful savage whom he knew to be one of the worst desperadoes and best marksmen in Captain Jack's band. In desperation he shouted, "Come on, boys! We can't let him go down there alone! They'll kill him sure!"

Swinging into their saddles, they were off, and soon arrived at the camp below, just in time to see One-Arm Brown closing in on Hooker Jim and demanding that he surrender. Applegate shouted, "Put up your gun!" then rode between the two men. As other braves, most of whom Applegate knew, came running from their lodges, Hooker Jim stood regarding him belligerently with piercing, bullet-like eyes, his teeth gleaming white in a leering grimace. In the language the Modocs knew best, the young subagent explained that they were there for peace, not war; that he had been sent to take them to Yainax where everything had been prepared for their arrival . . . where they would be under their old Chief, Schonchin.

The braves seemed favorably impressed and many of

them shook hands with Applegate. Some, however, held themselves aloof, waiting to see what was going to happen in Captain Jack's camp. As they watched, the figure of an Indian .... that of Scarface Charley, who had probably been out fishing .... paddled noiselessly down the river in a dugout canoe, then slipped up the bank unseen by the soldiers. When he reached the top, he let out a wild whoop that brought all those who had not already gathered running from their lodges.

Captain Jackson quickly ordered Scarface and the newcomers to drop their guns. After questioning glances at Captain Jack and the others, they did so, but Scarface kept his revolver and refused to give it up.

"You got my gun," he protested. "You let me keep pistol, me no shoot you."

Captain Jackson ordered Lieutenant Boutelle, who stood in advance of the line, to disarm him. Boutelle, gun in hand, turned to Scarface with the words, "Here you damn Injun, give me that pistol and be damn quick about it."

"Me no dog!" Scarface retorted angrily. "You no get him, my pistol!"

Boutelle advanced threateningly and Scarface whipped out his revolver and fired. Boutelle pressed the trigger of his gun so nearly at the same instant that only a single report rang out. Scarface Charley's bullet cut a long slit in Boutelle's coat sleeve, just above the elbow, and two holes in his shirt. Boutelle's shot pierced a red bandana that Scarface was wearing around his head. Neither man was injured.

These shots were the opening guns of the Modoc war. A wild melee ensued as the Modoc warriors piled on top of each other in a scramble to recover their guns, and the cavalrymen struggled to get their frightened horses under control. Captain Jackson shouted above the din and confusion the command, "Fire!" The troopers poured a volley of bullets into the midst of the Modocs who ran for cover. Shots came from everywhere . . . the sagebrush to the right, the river bank to the left, and from behind and within the lodges.

Men fell in the line. Riderless horses kicked frantically among the troopers. Captain Jackson's voice rang out, "Charge them, boys!" The soldiers rushed the whooping Indians, bringing down one of them, but the remainder slipped through the sagebrush, and came up from the rear. Bewildered by this fierce counterattack, the boys in blue faltered, and it seemed for a moment that the weakened line would break. But under the courageous leadership of their officers, they rallied and forced the redskins into retreat.

As if the shots of Boutelle and Scarface Charley had been a signal, Hooker Jim's braves on the east side of the river fired on the volunteers. A fierce hand to hand fight raged for a few minutes, but the Indians were too quick for the white men. After inflicting what damage they could, they made a desperate dash, reached their ponies tethered nearby, and escaped along a rocky ridge where pursuit would have been hopeless. Behind them they left one white man dead, one hopelessly maimed and several injured men, whom their comrades carried to Crawley's cabin where first aid was administered.

On the west side of the river the firing abated as the Modocs retreated, carrying with them the one Indian who had been killed. A quick check revealed several soldiers dead, about a dozen fatally wounded, and many others less seriously injured. Captain Jackson realized that, with so very few able-bodied soldiers left, there was no possibility of capturing the Modocs for they had scattered in the sagebrush. Nevertheless, he held the camp and everything in it, and ordered some of the men to set fire to it.

While the flames crackled and dense clouds of smoke rose from the burning lodges, the soldiers picked up their dead and wounded, placing them in the Indians' dugout canoes in which they were rowed across the river to be given care in the cabin with the other men. Captain Jackson divided what remained of his troop, leaving about ten men under Lieutenant Boutelle to hold the camp. The rest mounted their jaded horses for a seven mile ride to the nearest ford where they could cross the river, and return to Crawley's cabin to give protection to those taking refuge there in case of attack.

Dashing through the swirling waters, the horses seemed to realize the urgency of the situation. They put forth their utmost speed, and the exhausted cavalry squad came upon the scene of the fight between the volunteers and Hooker Jim's warriors, just in time to see Captain Jack lead his infuriated braves in a renewed attack on Boutelle and his pitifully few men. They watched helplessly as their comrades across the river engaged the redskins in what seemed to be a losing battle . . . and, no doubt, would have been, had the Modocs not run out of ammunition. As it was, a lusty cheer rose from the men at Crawley's cabin as Boutelle's troopers sent the Indians once more scurrying for the sagebrush where they were seen to mount their ponies and ride south, along the west shore of Tule lake.

If the soldiers had only known that the Indians were heading for their "stronghold" in the Lava Beds, the rendezvous where they had previously agreed to meet Hooker Jim and his braves in case they were separated by an attack, the troopers would have spared no effort to head them off. But they did not know, and instead breathed a sigh of relief that the Indians had gone, so they could give attention to the wounded. Even so, they did not relax their vigilance, for they fully expected an attack from Hooker Jim's warriors any moment.

Meanwhile, these same braves were holding a council in which the part the civilians had played in the fight, brought fiery words of indignation. The reason was that a few days previously the Modocs had elicted from the settlers in the vicinity of Tule lake, a promise that they would not take arms against the Indians in case they were attacked by the soldiers. They felt that they had been betrayed, probably not noting in the confusion, that the parties to the agreement were not involved in the battle. The high tension of the council talk was increased still further by the lust for blood, encouraged in these semi-savages by the life that they had taken.

But verbal reprisals were not sufficient. These must be translated into action, and there was not a dissenting voice when the proposal was made that they leave a bloody trail on their way to the Lava Beds by slaughtering the settlers. Their women and children were left to take a more round-about trail, while the infuriated Indians spurred their ponies toward the ranches of the stock men in a frenzy of excitement and revenge.

The first man they encountered was shot down in cold blood. Bruising and hacking the man's body, Hooker Jim stripped it and galloped up to the ranch house, where he boastingly flaunted the blood-soaked clothes before the man's wife, Mrs. Boddy.

"This is Boddy's blood!" he taunted. "But you no

be 'fraid. We are Modocs. We no kill women and children. You find your man in woods. We no hurt you!"

Paralyzed with terror, Mrs. Boddy watched Hooker Jim and several others who had joined him as they ransacked her home, taking all the money, guns and ammunition they could find.

In their mania for slaughter, this band of outlaws rode on from cabin to cabin, butchering every man they met, regardless of whether he had been a former friend or enemy. Even Henry Miller, who had supplied Hooker Jim with food and ammunition but a few days previously, was pierced through the heart by a bullet from Hooker's own gun. By the time they joined Captain Jack at the stronghold in the Lava Beds, the bodies of Brotherton, Schira, Schroeder and more than a dozen other men lay dead behind them.

Through the bitter cold and blackness of the night that followed, some of the braver women, wives of murdered men, made their way through the timber and sagebrush to Linkville with news of the fiendish massacre. These vivid accounts of the day and night of horrors, spread panic among the less courageous men, but the majority of them grimly determined to avenge the loss and suffering of the women, even at the cost of their lives.

Without delay, parties of stern-faced, well-armed men, set out for Tule lake with wagons to recover the bodies of those who had been massacred and at the same time, bring their stricken families to safety.

At the edge of a grove, they found Brotherton, his body pierced by four Modoc bullets, his glassy eyes wide open. Near him lay his axe, the handle and blade spattered with his own blood. Another victim hung face downward across the coupling poles of his wagon, where he had fallen. Still another, they located a few rods from his work, his body stripped of clothing and brutally dismembered.

Up and down the length of Tule lake, these men went on their tragic mission until eighteen gruesomely mutilated bodies lay side by side in the wagons. From the isolated farm houses, other teamsters gathered up the women and children who were exhausted by terror and grief. To those who had borne the brunt of suffering, it seemed as if it was the end of everything . . . but to those who saw their suffering, it was only the beginning.

CHAPTER VI

WAR MEDICINE

THE little village of Linkville fairly seethed with excitement. News of the battle and its indecisive outcome had created a state of tension among the stockmen and townspeople that broke loose in a sort of madness when they saw with their own eyes the mangled bodies of the massacred settlers . . . men who had been their friends. The word on every lip was war! war! war!

While couriers rode their horses to the limit, carrying messages urging an influx of soldiers and military equipment into the Modoc country, a little band of Hot Creek Modocs were preparing to leave their homes near the foot of the mountains which separated the Modoc country from the Shasta country to the south. They had no connection whatever with Captain Jack's renegades, having lived peacefully for many years on land adjacent to the J. F. ranch, owned by a stockman who had early learned that, when treated fairly, the Indians made good neighbors. This man was John Fairchild. He and a fellow stockman, Press Dorris, were held in high respect by the Hot Creeks, having made a practice of paying them a small compensation for land used for grazing the large herds of horses and cattle they had brought into the country.

The imminence of open hostilities between the whites and Captain Jack's band led Fairchild to suggest to the Hot Creeks that he and Dorris would guarantee them safe conduct to the reservation if they would go there to stay until peace was restored. Since the Hot Creeks had no desire to be implicated in Captain Jack's activities, they agreed. Accordingly, Fairchild sent a message to L. S. Dyer, who had succeeded Knapp as agent on the reservation, requesting him to meet the little party with a small cavalry escort at a ferry on Klamath river not far from Lower Klamath lake.

Somehow, the irate Linkville townspeople got wind of this maneuver. That these Indians were in no way involved in the Lost river and the Tule lake depredations made no difference to them. Their animosities were aroused and they were determined to exterminate any and every Modoc they could find.

Even before the slight, gray-haired Dyer had arrived at Linkville, a party of lynch-minded citizens were on their way to the ferry crossing on the Klamath river. There, the first man they met was John Fairchild, whose sandy hair and bushy eyebrows fairly bristled with anger when he heard their demand that he turn the Hot Creek Indians over to them.

Fairchild's piercing, steel-gray eyes raked them with the utmost contempt. He let flow a stream of language from his caustic tongue that fairly caused the men before him to shrink visibly. Not for an instant did his hand leave the butt of the revolver in his holster. His reputation as a sharpshooter plus the unflinching presence of Press Dorris, lent conviction to the words with which he battered the ears of his listeners.

They tried to retaliate, but Fairchild's nimble tongue gave him all the advantage and the would-be lynchers finally rode off, their figurative tails between their legs. This seemed to settle matters, but things had been happening elsewhere.

When Fairchild and Dorris again turned their attention to the Indians, they were nowhere to be found. They had seen and heard what had been going on, and the demonstration of the intensity of feeling in Linkville frightened them thoroughly. Rather than pass through the town, they had stampeded and headed straight for the Lava Beds, adding fourteen more braves to those already under the leadership of Captain Jack.

Fairchild was furious to find that his efforts had been so completely frustrated. Moreover, he knew that the Linkville trouble-makers had been responsible for gratuitously placing no mean force at Captain Jack's command. There was Shacknasty Jim, the origin of whose name was associated with his mother's housekeeping. He was a finely built young fellow whose tough, sinewy body and sharpshooting ability belied his somewhat feminine features which were emphasized by his light complexion, and hair parted in the middle. Steamboat Frank was another one of these Hot Creek Indians, so named because of his wife's great size and her habit of puffing and blowing. Fairchild knew that he was a formidable antagonist, when angered. Then there was Ellen's Man, little more than an over-grown boy with a full-moon face, who had been adopted as a lad by a squaw much older than he was, who later married him. Although rather simple-minded, he could be depended upon to fight with a stubborn determination that amounted to recklessness.

These three, particularly, and the eleven other Hot Creek braves were to add greatly to the difficulties encountered by the white men before they saw the end of the Modoc trouble. At the end of their hurried flight across the hills and plateaus from Lower Klamath lake, they were welcomed by the other Modocs, who were preparing to defend their "stronghold" against any attack.

This "stronghold" was located in the midst of volcanic terrain composed of fractured lava rock, giving the appearance of a tumultuous sea that had suddenly crystallized at the height of its greatest commotion. There was no vegetation, except clumps of sagebrush and bunch grass, that, somehow, managed to eke out a living from the crevices of those barren rocks.

Surrounding a crater-like pit, big enough for a large house to drop into it with room to spare, were great fissures and caverns, which formed a network of natural trenches and "dugouts" hard to surpass. Here and there rocks were piled up in semi-circular fashion with loop holes left for the muzzles of guns. The Indians had built these breastworks with their own hands to fill in the few gaps left by nature in their fortifications.

The only comparatively easy access to this natural fortress was a rough, jagged trail, leading from the edge of Tule lake, about three-quarters of a mile away, the lake being their only source of water. Guarding this trail were craggy outcroppings, which rose for some distance on either side of it, like teeth of immense crosscut saws. These spikes of lava offered perfect protection, for a hundred yards or more, to anyone who might be passing along the trail. This path, so cleverly hidden and protected, came out at last, by devious windings to the stronghold in which Captain Jack and his braves had chosen to defend themselves. Here was a refuge perfectly adapted to the purpose, forming a fortress practically impregnable to either infantry or cavalry, no matter how strong.

While the Modocs were consolidating their forces, military preparations were moving forward rapidly. At Fort Klamath and at Linkville the winter sun gleamed on the polished trappings of officers, and glittered on the bayonets of privates. Heated conversations and martial music filled the air as troops poured in from every available source.

Within a month after the battle on Lost river, four hundred armed men were closing in on Captain Jack's band of fifty warriors in the Lava Beds. About two hundred and fifty of these men were "regulars" under the command of General Frank Wheaton; one hundred and twenty were Oregon volunteer militiamen under General J.E. Ross; and twenty-five belonged to an independent company of California volunteers of whom John Fairchild was made captain.

The Oregon militia, which was placed under the direct command of General Wheaton, was divided into two companies. Harrison Kelly was selected as captain of one of these divisions, and Oliver Applegate was captain of the other. About twenty of the sixty men under Captain Applegate's command were Klamath scouts, who welcomed the opportunity to pay off their old grudges against the Modocs by helping the white men. In order to distinguish them from the enemy, they were provided with white badges to wear on non-regulation army caps.

These forces were concentrated in two camps, one

under the command of Colonel Barnard at the south
end of Tule lake, five or six miles almost due east of
Captain Jack's stronghold; the other was under General Wheaton at Van Bremer's ranch, about fifteen
miles due west, separated from the lake and the Lava
Beds by a series of ridges and plateaus. The only route
of communication between the two camps was by a
rough, corkscrew trail called Ticknor road which circled the Lava Beds on the south, or by a wide detour
around Tule lake on the north. The Tule lake route
was more easily travelled and was the one used most.

Over these roads, and others leading from Fort
Klamath in Oregon and Fort Bidwell in California,
jolted wagons loaded with supplies of food, clothing
and fighting equipment for the two army camps. Since
the Indians were badly in need of replenishing their
guns and ammunition, they lost no opportunity to hold
up and rob these wagon-trains.

On December 21, one Saturday morning, a government supply train from Fort Bidwell, escorted by six
soldiers, was nearing Colonel Barnard's camp when the
Indians struck. Hidden behind the rocks beside the
road, their guns barked without warning, and before
the party could locate a target to shoot at, five horses
and two soldiers lay dead, four others being severely
injured. This occurred so close to Barnard's camp that
the shots were heard, and the colonel rushed his men
hurriedly to the rescue, but arrived too late. They
found two of the dead men scalped, the supplies of
ammunition gone and not an Indian in sight.

Early in January another wagon was attacked in a
similar fashion, but with fewer casualties. The first shot
from the redskins grazed one of the mules, warning
the driver, who whipped up his team, and went bounc-

ing along over the rocky road with the Modoc bullets
whistling around him. The largest part of his load
was jolted overboard and scattered along the road behind him, where the attackers picked it up, obtaining
several canteens, a case of whiskey and more ammunition. That night the men in Colonel Barnard's camp
looked on ruefully as the Indians built a great fire on
an elevation not over a quarter of a mile away and celebrated their success by a war dance.

But the repeated attacks on the supply wagons didn't
dampen the spirits of the majority of the soldiers and
volunteers, especially in the camp at Van Bremer's
which was too far away from the Lava Beds to be
directly molested by marauders. Their greatest fear
was that the fight wouldn't last long enough for everyone to win distinction.

In the midst of all the talk of victory, only General
Wheaton, Colonel John Green and Captain Jackson, all
veteran officers, were dubious. Perhaps, their talks with
John Fairchild and Press Dorris had something to do
with it. These men knew the Modocs, they knew the
Lava Beds. They had hunted cattle all over this country, and knew the lay of it better than any other white
men in camp.

One of the captains of volunteers said to Fairchild,
"You know, there's only one thing I'm worrying about
and that is that I won't be able to restrain my men.
They're eager to get at 'em! Why, if I let 'em go,
they'd eat the Modocs up raw!"

"Don't fret yourself," Fairchild's quick tongue replied. "You won't have no trouble holdin' 'em. They
won't be a bit hard to keep back when the Modocs open
fire!"

To some of the other men, who were airing their impatience, he said, caustically, "Never you fear! You'll have plenty on your hands before your mothers see you again. Them Modocs are sure rarin' and they sure know how to rare!"

Other such remarks could be heard among the men in uniforms.

"I say, Jim, are we goin' to take any grub with us?"

"Hell no!" was the reply. "We're goin' to have Modoc steaks for dinner tomorrow night!"

"An' I'm thinkin'," chimed in another, "That I'll be takin' mine rare!"

A third man insisted that he was going to capture a good looking squaw . . . . for a dishwasher. One young man with stripes on his sleeves announced his intention to take home some little Injuns for servants. Several of them got into a heated argument over who was going to take possession of Captain Jack's "pacin' hoss."

But as Friday, January 17, the day set for the attack on the stronghold drew nearer, the men had little time for talk as every effort was concentrated on drills, mimic charges and the march to the bluff above the Lava Beds from which the offensive was to start.

Rations for three days were issued on Thursday and the troops, marching light, began their trek directly across the rugged country which separated them from Captain Jack's stronghold. They arrived at the top of the bluff about 1:00 o'clock Thursday. The supply wagons, however, had to take a round-about road to the north and did not arrive until about dark.

Just about sundown on the eve of the battle, General Wheaton and Captain Jackson stood with field glasses in hand at the edge of the plateau that dropped abruptly away to the Lava Beds and the Modoc country to the northeast. They presented a strange contrast, these two men: Wheaton short, slight, with sharp sensitive features and Jackson ruggedly built and ruddy faced. Together they scanned in minute detail all that could be seen from their vantage spot.

As their glasses swung from right to left, Jackson kept up a running fire of comment regarding the historic spots on which they gazed. Captain Jack's present hideout, the neat white rows of tents, forming Colonel Barnard's camp, the deserted ranch houses of massacred settlers, Bloody Point, Captain Jack's Lost river camp, and the scene of the Ben Wright massacre . . . all these claimed their attention.

But as if drawn by an invisible force, their eyes rested once more on the stronghold of Captain Jack, and Colonel Barnard's camp. "Those white tents look like playthings, even under a field glass, don't they?" General Wheaton observed.

"Well, they're farther away than you'd think . . . maybe six or seven miles," Jackson replied. "I hope they don't have any trouble picking up our signals in the morning . . . if it doesn't turn off clear, we'll be up against it! I don't know of any other way we can be sure that our combined forces will move on the Modocs at the same time, do you?"

"No, we'll have to depend on the signals. It *must* be clear. It's bad enough to fight in a country like this under the best conditions, but in such a fog as I've heard they often have here, it would be next to hopeless!"

"Those fogs are thick, all right. It's just like being packed in cotton," Jackson said. "It'd be mighty easy to get lost . . . " Although his voice stopped, he was evidently engaged in following the thought, as the two officers gazed out across the great valley stretching southward from the deeply indented shore line of Tule lake. To the naked eye, the country seemed smooth and flat, which it was far from being. Near the far boundary of this plain, they could see four buttes standing in a line like sentinels. Far beyond, hoary-headed Mt. Shasta loomed, overlooking the country for miles on every side.

"We can't afford to get lost, no matter what the conditions are," Wheaton mused at last. "Too much depends on the outcome of tomorrow's battle with these redskins. If we don't come back victorious . . . well, no two ways about it. We must win!"

Dusk was creeping over the Lava Beds, a dusk that brought forbidding shadows. At the sound of mess call, the two officers mounted their horses and rode back to camp. After the evening meal, the officers held a brief conference, stationed a guard for the night, and soon quiet reigned throughout the hopeful camp.

But in the stronghold a few miles away, there was everything but rest and quiet. That night the Modocs, except a few who were stationed on sentinel duty, gathered around the fire in a solemn war council. Fifty warriors, about half of them in "Boston dress" as they called white men's clothes, and the rest in savage costume, squatted tensely and expectantly as the fire cast weird shadows upon their faces.

While the war council was going on, the Modoc women were pressed into service. Some stood immobile, staring sphinx-like at the ramparts above the stronghold. Despite appearances, they were keenly alert. This outlaw band felt reasonably sure that they were safe from the observation of the palefaces, yet they were taking no chances on being surprised. Other women of the tribe had been assigned the work of gathering sagebrush to replenish the fire to keep its flames shooting high.

Every Modoc in camp was waiting for their Chief to signal that the war-council was ready to begin. As the fire was burning brightly, and the stir caused by late-comers had subsided, Captain Jack arose and stood in silent dignity. He looked searchingly from face to face in the circle around him before he finally spoke.

"We are Modocs," he said, speaking slowly in the ancient language of the tribe. "We are brave and strong. But our numbers are few. We do wrong to fight the white man. Suppose we kill all the soldiers. More will take their places. When a Modoc dies, no one can come to take his place. I don't want war. I don't want to fight men who have been our friends. I say let us live in peace with the white man."

This speech was the signal for others to voice their opinions. Schonchin John stood up. His deeply seamed face was set in lines of hatred and revenge. He spoke rapidly, contentiously.

"Maybe we die," he almost shouted. "But we no die first. We will kill many white men. We no give up." He recalled the Ben Wright affair and warned his tribesmen that they could expect nothing but treachery from the palefaces.

When he had finished, Scarface Charley arose to speak. "I was mad on Lost river," he said. "My blood was hot. They called me bad names and I got red-hot like fire. Now I see different. Many white men are my friends. I no want to kill them. I am not afraid. My heart is strong. But the Modocs are few and the white men are many. Our Chief speaks well. We cannot whip the white men. I don't want war. But what the heart of our people is, my heart is. I am a Modoc."

While these Indians spoke, the perpetual scowl on Curly Head Doctor's face had been getting deeper and blacker. As their medicine man, he had the complete confidence of practically all of the tribe, and an overbearing cocksureness in his powers. He had been with Hooker Jim and the murdering gang who had terrorized the settlers along the shore of Tule lake, and his lust for blood had not abated during the intervening weeks.

Rising to speak, he sent a fearless, defiant look at Captain Jack and then began to speak in a voice that was clear and commanding: "My hands are red with white men's blood. When I saw our women and children killed on Lost river, I was mad. I wanted to kill all white men. The more white men to kill the better. They cannot fight. Palefaces shoot in the air. We are not tired. We are not yellow dogs. We won't give up! We want war! Curly Head Doctor, he make medicine that will turn white man's bullets away from Modocs. Then we kill all that come!" With a decisive gesture, he sat down, certain that he could do as he promised.

When the discussion finally ended, Captain Jack announced that the matter would be put to a vote. All those who were in favor of war would gather around Schonchin John and Curly Head Doctor, those who were for peace would line up with their Chief and Scarface Charley.

The warriors rose from their squatting positions and milled to the side with which they wished to cast their lot. For several minutes, uncertainty reigned. But when the two groups were counted, the verdict was overwhelming. War was the answer!

Only fourteen braves out of the fifty who had participated in the council had dared to stand out for peace, while the thirty-six bloodthirsty redskins who held the balance of power were determined to fight to the finish.

The clear, logical reasoning of Captain Jack and Scarface Charley couldn't compete with Curly Head Doctor's promise that he would perform a magic that would turn the bullets of the white men from the Modocs. With this protection assured them, the majority of the tribe were ready to take any chances, no matter how foolhardy.

The medicine man was exultant over the results of the vote. He immediately retired to his cave to begin preparation for fulfilling his promise. First, he prepared roots and meats, putting them through processes designed to make them especially attractive to Kamoo-cum-chux. Then he called together the women of the band, whom he ordered to build a ceremonial fire. Going through many rites and gesticulations, he placed the sacrifices of roots and meats on the red hot embers and waited for the smoke and odor of burning food to permeate the air. Inhaling vigorously, he began his incantations.

He called loudly upon the spirits of dead warriors and invoked the assistance of the Great Spirit in behalf of his tribe. Pitching a tune to his words, the Indian women accompanied him in a weird chant, which rose louder and louder, as they circled 'round and 'round with jerky, bent-kneed hop-steps, their shoulders touching. The rhythm was marked by resonant sounds that came from the activities of a drummer, who swayed back and forth, as he beat on a drumhead of dried rawhide which was drawn tightly over a rough-made hoop.

On and on went the singing dancers, the voices of both the medicine man and the squaws rising to a higher and higher pitch, as the excitement grew in intensity. The braves did not participate in this ceremony, but crowded close to see what prospects the medicine making seemed to indicate. The dancers were carried away in the frenzy of the moment, but at last, utterly exhausted, they felt assured of the presence of the spirits they had summoned.

Meanwhile Captain Jack had returned to his cave where he sat gravely mapping out his plans for the coming battle. When the rest of the braves returned from the medicine dance, he assigned each man to a particular station, appointing certain women to carry water and ammunition. Others he instructed to mold lead into bullets for the old-fashioned octagonal small bore muskets, which were the principal weapons in possession of the Modocs. Turning from these tasks, he inspected the guns and ammunition, estimating how long the latter would hold out.

When everything was in readiness for the attack which they expected at any time, the Indians went off to their own caves to sleep, leaving only the sentinels and Captain Jack to wait through a long, wakeful night for what the dawn might bring.

CHAPTER VII

BATTLING IN HADES

CLEAR, cold blackness still surrounded General Wheaton's camp on the bluff at the edge of the Lava Beds when reveille sounded at 4:00 o'clock on the morning of January 17. Shivering men threw aside their blankets, dressed hastily and reported at the mess tent for their rations of hard tack and coffee. Some of them squatted on their heels as they ate, but most of them, cup in one hand and hard tack in the other, kept on the move in an effort to keep warm.

Even before they had all finished eating, the order to "fall in" rang out from the bugles. The blue-uniformed men lined up like automatons with the precision of long practice. Beside them, the ranks of volunteers looked most unmilitary in their miscellaneous civilian clothes. As the roll was called, shouts, "Here!" "Here!" "Here!" echoed down the lines.

General Wheaton, a small dynamo of energy, stood before his men. They were orderly and confident, eager to get under way. So sure was he of a brief, successful campaign that he ordered the troops to travel light, carrying only a small bit of food for lunch. He spoke pointedly, saying that he expected them to return from the Modoc stronghold with every redskin either dead or captured.

When the troops started the march to the edge of the bluff, it was not yet light, and the stars shone in cold, wintry brightness from a clear sky. By the time the men reached the brink of the cliff, the first streaks of a cloudless dawn had begun to show in the east.

The apparent ideal weather conditions early that morning left the troops wholly unprepared for the sight that confronted them, as they looked down into the valley below. A billowy white mass hid everything but the tops of the higher buttes. With dismay, they realized that what they saw was the upper side of a dense bank of fog.

Consternation swept over officers and men alike. Every one of them understood how disastrous the fog was to their chances of success. The ocean of mist, which concealed the black sweep of rocks and gave the lie to their senses, also gave protection to the Modocs.

The men in command held a hurried consultation. This unexpected barrier made the howitzers useless for bombarding the stronghold, since no target was visible at which to aim. Their means of signaling Colonel Barnard, whose attack from the east would be left unsupported unless the plans previously arranged were followed, was cut off. There seemed to be no alternative but to advance.

Accordingly orders were given that started the regulars and volunteers single file down the narrow, precipitous trail into the Lava Beds. As they went, the men at the head of the line appeared to those behind to be swallowed up by some fantastic monster. When the troops had all reached the fairly level ground at the bottom, they spread out in close skirmish formation and prepared for offensive movement.

"Forward .... March!" General Wheaton's sharp order was muffled by the heavy mist. The bugle repeated the command, but even its usual clearness was dulled.

Directly into the fog-haunted Lava Beds the line advanced. At first it moved forward as one man, but soon became disorganized and irregular, one end of the line being invisible to the other. Rocks and chasms which had to be surmounted or detoured blocked the way, making the advance laborious and difficult. Gradually even the sense of direction became uncertain.

The regulars, especially those who had done battle with the Modocs at Lost river, advanced slowly, reluctantly. The volunteers seemed "rarin' to go." Frequently Fairchild called to his men, "Go slow, boys! Go slow! We'll raise 'em soon enough and no mistake!"

A few miles away to the east, Colonel Barnard's troops were moving in raggedly, hindered by the same obstacles and hemmed in by the same low-lying fog. Nevertheless, the net around the Modoc stronghold was tightening. Soon the two lines would execute a half-wheel that would bring together their southern ends, then it would be only a short time before Captain Jack and his band would beg for mercy. At least the bluecoats and volunteers thought so.

But the fifty redskin warriors, who were fighting for their very existence thought differently. When they saw the fog rolling in, they were exuberant. To them it was the answer to the medicine-making of the night before. It was the "magic" that Curly Head Doctor had promised them to turn the white man's bullets away; a sign from Ka-moo-cum-chux that he would protect his people and bring them victory.

Although this "magic" obliterated familiar landmarks, these rock-dwellers had no need of them for they knew this country as a tiger knows his own den. While the soldiers cursed the fog for increasing the difficulty of making a successful attack, the Modoc scouts rejoiced, for they were enabled to follow every movement of the enemy without themselves being seen.

So as the net closed in, Captain Jack and his warriors were fully prepared. Each brave was at his station, well-concealed behind protective rocks with the barrel of his gun thrust through a crevice, waiting for the first paleface-target to appear, no matter how dimly through the mist.

Back among the military ranks, the men were becoming impatient as they stumbled on through a seemingly endless stretch of fog and over rocks without so much as a glimpse of an Indian. Some became convinced that the Modocs had deserted their position.

"Yeah, I knew they'd leave when they found us volunteers was after 'em!" one man growled.

"Just you show me an Injun and I'll show you a dead one!" boasted another.

The broken line of troops had not gone more than fifty yards when a rumble like a stampede of cattle rolled and echoed across the rocks. They halted involuntarily, for they knew it was the sound of firing, muffled by fog and distance.

The line surged forward. A cheer arose among the men as the suspense of the deadening silence was broken.

"Barnard's opened on 'em. Now we'll go!" shouted someone.

"Hurrah! We'll take 'em from the rear! Hurrah! Hurrah! Hurrah for Hell!"

"Yeah, three cheers for the country you're goin' to!" cut in a less enthusiastic comrade.

On into the dense fog the men plunged. Just then, a faint spurt of fire leapt out of the mist in front of Captain Kelly's company. A bullet whistled through the air. This time the sound was sharp and clear. The soldiers' cheers stuck in their throats, as they stood for a moment, tense and rigid, trying to make out the direction from which it came. As they hesitated a volunteer fell, rolling crazily before their eyes on the sharp rocks, writhing with pain.

"Damn your eyes!" he shouted. "Get me out of here! Can't you see I'm shot? My thigh's broke!"

Two men hurried to assist him. As they lifted the wounded man a withering volley of lead seemed to be centered on them from every direction. They sought cover, but one of them fell .... fell and was unable to rise again.

The confusion produced by this sudden Modoc onslaught vanished, as the undaunted Colonel Green rallied the men with the command "Fire!" All along the line a blaze of light burst forth and the fight was on.

"Charge!" shouted the colonel. "Charge" repeated the bugle. The line pressed forward double-quick over the uncertain footing of jagged rocks and treacherous holes. For a hundred yards they stumbled on, the Modoc bullets thinning their ranks. They emptied their guns time after time, yet their shots went wild, glancing off rocks to fall ineffectively. Straining their eyes to pierce the dense fog, they could find no targets for their bullets.

After several hours of continuous battle, the enemy's firing quieted, then the soldiers felt encouraged. "They've beat it!" shouted an exultant voice. But the words were drowned out by the Modoc war-whoops, shrill enough to curdle men's blood. More troopers fell, but their comrades charged savagely and forced the redskins back.

About eleven o'clock, Captain Perry, in obedience to an order from Colonel Green, changed the position of his company from Captain Applegate's right to connect with Captain Kelly's left, in order to relieve temporarily those who had borne the brunt of the morning's fighting. The dense fog had not yet lifted, but the line moved steadily on, stumbling into treacherous fissures that yawned beneath them, climbing painfully out over sharp-edged rocks that cut their shoes and left their hands lacerated and bloody.

Yet it was not the pitfalls and holes the soldiers feared so much as the open spaces. Out in the open, they were mowed down by unseen Modoc marksmen who seemed to have no end to the rocky defenses to which they could fall back. As a result, the troops suffered severely in killed and wounded without being able to inflict any serious injury upon the enemy.

All during the early afternoon the troops drove on through this inferno, intent upon making the junction with Colonel Barnard's line at the south of the stronghold. In a desperate effort to accomplish this end, Colonel Green fearlessly leapt onto a jutting embankment of rocks. "Forward, men!" he shouted. "Mount the ridge!"

The first man to obey the command staggered back under the impact of a Modoc bullet. Still Green stood his ground, as a dozen rifles in unseen hands hailed lead around him.

"Come on! Up men! Up and over!" Another man reeled and fell. "It's our one chance! Give 'em all you got, boys!" the intrepid colonel urged. Other bluecoats responded only to fall back. The heap of dead and wounded at the base of the ridge grew, as one by one, those attempting to make it were picked off by the Modoc sharpshooters. Yet Green stood as if protected by a charm, the bullets whistling ineffectively around him until he was finally forced by the casualties among his men to drop back.

A hasty consultation of officers led to the decision to give up the attempt to join the lines at the south, instead making a flank movement to the left that would bring the lines together on the lake side of the stronghold. About three o'clock this movement began with Captain Fairchild's company in advance.

In order to accomplish the junction, the troops would have to pass under a point of rocks, projecting close to the lake shore. It was completely enveloped in fog, alive with Indians, whose sharpshooters could easily bring down anyone attempting to pass. Nevertheless, Fairchild's company charged forward. Where the lead rained fastest, two men fell wounded. Fairchild called a halt in an attempt to remove the injured to safety rather than leave them to the mercy of the redskins. Their only hope was to drag the two men to a small recess under the overhanging rocks, which they accomplished successfully. There they were able to keep out of range of enemy bullets, and at the same time, compel the Indians to keep their distance while

Captain Perry's and Captain Mason's regulars passed the point in comparative safety.

Colonel Barnard, wounded but still going, tried to drive back the Indians until Fairchild's company could complete the passage with their injured men, but reinforcements for the redskins had come up and made the maneuver impossible. In the niche under the rocky point the men were forced to lie flat on the ground among the sharp rocks to keep out of range of Captain Jack's warriors. Even with the utmost precaution, however, one of the men fell a victim to a Modoc bullet. Relief being impossible, the cold-numbed volunteers determined to hold their precarious position until nightfall, when they could take their dead and wounded and join Colonel Barnard's command.

Shortly before five o'clock, the fog lifted for a few minutes, disclosing a watery sun rapidly sinking behind Mt. Shasta. The soldiers realized that darkness would soon be upon them and all their day of blind battling would have been in vain. Discouraged, weary, their spirits broken, the men stumbled forward, half-heartedly.

Suddenly a concentrated volley of Modoc fire caused the line now nearest the lake to fall back. A sort of panic swept, from man to man, down the fast thinning ranks. General Wheaton, fearful that the Modocs might make a night assault on his command, was forced to admit that there was no use trying to push the attack further. He took advantage of the brief interval during which the fog lifted to signal Colonel Barnard to withdraw his forces, take a new position that he could hold during the night, and then return to camp the next day.

He ordered his own men to "Cease firing!" The

bugles sounded retreat. Silently, bitterly conscious of their defeat, the soldiers began to retrace their steps, fearful that at any moment they might have to meet a counter attack by the Indians. The wounded, to whom the meaning of the bugle call was all too clear, shouted to their comrades not to leave them for the Modocs to take as prisoners.

Some of the volunteers halted, and returned to aid the wounded men. Reaching one of them, two of the rescuers started to lift him up, when a bullet struck one of the men, and he dropped beside his wounded comrade. Others tried to return to bring the two help-less men to safety. Crawling on their hands and knees, they had almost reached the disabled ones, when an-other man crumpled before their eyes. The task was hopeless.

One of the wounded soldiers begged the volunteers to shoot him. "Don't leave me alive for those Modoc devils!" he cried. "Shoot me! Shoot now! My God, don't let them take me alive!"

But the routed army was in retreat, and the war-whoops and bullets of the Modocs prevented them from giving aid to those left behind. Soon they were out of hearing of the cries of pain and terror that arose from their doomed comrades, as night settled down over a bloody battlefield.

Groping their way through darkness, their feet bleeding where their shoes had been cut into ribbons by the knifelike sharpness of volcanic rock, the remnants of the army tramped half-heartedly back to the camp.

For ten hours these men, numbering into the hundreds, had fought fifty invisible foes. Fatigued almost beyond the point of endurance, and weak with hunger and cold, those who were alive climbed the trail back up the bluff, carrying the few dead and wounded they were able to retrieve.

The last soldiers to struggle up the steep trail long after darkness had fallen, gazed back upon a sight which intensified the rankling thought of their defeat. The fog, like a fiendish, shapeless monster, had rolled northward and settled at the far end of Tule lake. Now the reflections of the huge fire the Indians had built to celebrate their victory were visible.

Had the soldiers been closer, they could have seen the Modoc warriors gathered around the fire, exultant and boastful over their success. Every man was in his place, for the white men had not killed a single brave. There had not been so much as a serious injury to any of Captain Jack's men.

Curly Head Doctor, hero of the day, stood proudly before the Modoc warriors, bragging of his powers. "I promised you a medicine that would turn the white man's bullets," he said. "Where is the Modoc who has been killed? I told you Ka-moo-cum-chux, the Great Spirit, was with us. Your Chief's heart was weak. Mine was strong. We can kill all the white men that come!"

Schonchin John, too, took up the boast. "I felt strong when I saw the fog our medicine man brought over the rocks," he said as he grinned, showing yellow snags of teeth. "I knew we would kill the soldiers! We are Modocs!"

But there were a few who felt as Captain Jack did when he arose at the close of the council and said slowly, speaking the language they all knew. "It is true we have killed many white men. The Modoc heart is strong. The Modoc guns are sure. We are all here. But hear me, oh muck-a-lux (my people)! The white men are many. They will come again. No matter how many the Modocs kill, more will come. We will all be killed in the end!

"I am your voice. My blood is Modoc. I will not make peace until the Modoc heart says peace. But I know we will not live to see our Lost river country again, unless we can stop this war!"

He raised his hand as a signal that the council was at an end. The braves went on with their celebration, dancing and singing. But the general spirit of rejoicing seemed to have been noticeably tempered by Captain Jack's words, or, perhaps, by the fatigue of the day which was beginning to tell on them in spite of the exhilarating effect of victory.

CHAPTER VIII

HONOR AMONG SAVAGES

THE morning of January 18 found the braves out on the field of battle before sun-up, each one eager to out-do the other in the booty he could collect. With fiendish delight, they came upon the stiff, cold bodies of soldiers and volunteers, as well as a few who had managed to survive the night, nursing the agony of their wounds and fighting against hunger and cold. They ended the suffering of these terror-stricken men by stoning them to death. Then they stripped the corpses of clothing, arms and ammunition, scalped them and attached the coveted trophies to their belts. When they returned to camp, they were loaded down with loot, most important of which were the muskets and cartridge belts they had taken from the dead, and picked up where the troops had made their disorderly retreat.

By the time the scouting parties from the military camps reached the scene of the previous day's struggle, they found little left save the crushed and mutilated bodies of their comrades. Unmolested by the Indians, they carried as many as they could recover to the foot of the bluff where corpse after corpse was being lowered into the shallow graves dug for them.

All through the camp it was evident that the morale of the men had suffered a terrible blow. The high hopes held on the night before the battle were in such sharp contrast to the disillusionment of the day after that even the stoutest hearts found it impossible to remain unaffected by the sense of desperation that swept over the ranks. Their overwhelming defeat seemed impossible, fantastic. Yet as a silent reminder, the official announcement was posted, listing thirty-seven regulars and eleven volunteers killed or wounded.

In view of the demoralization of the troops and the difficulty of conquering the stronghold revealed by the unsuccessful attack, General Wheaton decided that it would be futile to attempt any further movement against the renegades until reinforcements, "at least a thousand men", had been stationed in the Modoc country. He ordered the camp moved back to the base at Van Bremer's ranch and the volunteers mustered out of service until they were needed again.

For a week after the battle, each night's roll-call revealed gaps in the ranks that could not be accounted for by death or injury. Desertion was the answer. The would-be steak-eaters couldn't stomach the idea of marching against those Modoc devils another time. "Better be a live coward than a dead hero" became a popular, although unexpressed sentiment.

Dissension arose among the officers. General Wheaton was denounced as incompetent. Steps were taken that resulted in his removal and General Frank Gillem was appointed to take his place.

The authorities at Washington, D. C. and every citizen in the country were electrified by the reports of this first major encounter with the Modocs in their own stronghold. On the face of it ... and the face of it was all they could see ... nothing could seem more absurd than that four hundred soldiers armed with the best guns and ammunition should suffer such a decisive defeat at the hands of fifty redskins, defending themselves with rusty muskets and hand-made bullets.

Everyone had an opinion to advance on the situation ... everyone, that is, except those who knew the conditions under which the battle had been fought. Most of these suggestions involved wholesale carnage and the word "annihilation" leapt into popular usage almost over night.

Those who knew the inside story of how the Modoc trouble had developed and the odds stacked against a successful government campaign were not so extravagant, either in thought or action. Aside from the indisputable fact that the Indians had the advantage of an almost impregnable stronghold to make up for their lack of numbers, the more fair-minded believed that Captain Jack also had a certain moral justification for the stand he had taken.

To this level-headed minority among the officials at Washington, D. C., the picture shaped up about like this. Here were two Indian tribes, the Klamaths and the Modocs. They had been at war for generations, having known each other always as ancient and irreconcilable enemies.

Suddenly the advent of the white men forced the Modocs to give up their tribal homes to be quartered on land the Klamaths had long claimed as theirs, even before the reservation was established. The Klamaths had openly persecuted the Modocs, robbing them of their rights while the government, which had promised to protect them, looked on and did nothing.

What else could be expected than the Modocs should do exactly as they had done? After all, they had simply returned to their former home, and in doing so, had become a nuisance to the white men who in the meantime had taken over their land.

Then, too, these renegade Indians had been promised a small reservation of their own on Lost river in order to quiet them. But since that was not forthcoming, they again became obnoxious to the settlers who tried to use force in herding them back onto Klamath reservation. Instead, they forced them into bloody deeds and a retreat in the Lava Beds where they resisted successfully the attack of four hundred soldiers.

Were they so much at fault? And whether they were or not, what was to be done? What could be done?

These were the questions which the officials in Washington D. C. asked themselves and they brought into focus the realization that, perhaps, a wrong had been done that could never be righted by force. Moreover, the fact must be faced that even if they chose to use force, success could only be attained by the expenditure of an enormous sum of money and great loss in human lives.

Other questions arose. Might not the war and bloodshed involved in such a course of action stir up trouble among the other Indians, who, so far, had accepted their new life on the reservation without protest? And even if the Modocs were finally beaten back onto the reservation against their will, how could they be kept there?

These were the factors that influenced the men in Washington to try the "pow-wow" method before again resorting to arms, on the premise that "jaw-bone" was cheaper than ammunition. A. B. Meacham, who had accomplished the seemingly impossible in getting Captain Jack's band back on the reservation in 1869, was in the capital at the time. His record for successful dealing with the renegades led to his appointment as peace commissioner. It was up to him, then, to try to adjust the difficulties of these now-desperate people.

He accepted the job with misgiving. It was a dangerous mission and he knew it. So did the others who were appointed to act under him. They were Samuel Case, then acting Indian agent at Alsea, Ore.; Jesse Applegate, a man of long frontier experience; and General Canby, who was to act as counselor for the group. With the slowness of transportation it was fully a month after the battle before the commissioners were all assembled at Van Bremer's ranch, ready to open negotiations.

There had been few contacts between the two enemy camps during that time, so the opening of communication with the Indians was their first task. For this purpose they secured the services of a "squaw-man," named Bob Whittle, and his Indian wife, instructing them to tell Captain Jack that the Great White Father had sent some of his chiefs to talk things over with him. If possible they were to arrange for a meeting.

These messengers well knew when they left the military camp on that raw February morning that the chances were against their safe return, yet, in true frontier fashion, they set out bravely against the greatest odds. The peace commissioners and soldiers anxiously watched the two mounted figures as their silhouettes against the skyline became smaller and smaller and at last disappeared.

The hours dragged endlessly, while the fate of those who had ventured into the Modoc stronghold hung in the balance. Toward evening, as the lengthening shadows had begun to increase the apprehension of the waiting commissioners, the messengers returned with the good news that the renegade band was willing to meet John Fairchild and Whittle at the edge of the Lava Beds for the purpose of arranging a "cultus wawa" with the peace men.

Next morning these two "ambassadors", accompanied by Whittle's wife and another squaw, met Captain Jack and several of his braves. In order to make an impression on the Modocs, Meacham had sent the following note which Fairchild read to Captain Jack and Whittle interpreted.

"To Captain Jack, Schonchin John and others:
"Captain Fairchild will talk for us a few things. We have come a long way to see you in behalf of the President and have brought you no bad words. Our instuctions say we must look into the trouble that caused the war. We want to hear both sides and then we can say to the President what we think is best. He wants us to write down all about it. What Mr. Fairchild says we will agree to, about when and where the talk will be held. It is a disgrace for either side to take advantage while we are fixing for a council. Our side will not move any soldiers or take any advantage. Ben Wright did wrong. The white men do not approve of such things. What our men agree to do they will stand by.
"A. B. Meacham,
"Chairman of the Peace Commission."

To this and Fairchild's explanation, Captain Jack replied, "I understand you about not fighting or killing cattle or stealing horses. Tell your people they needn't be afraid while we are making peace. My boys will stay in the rocks. We will not fire the first shot."

There followed several meetings of intermediaries in an effort to make arrangements satisfactory to both sides, but they all ended in a deadlock. The white men refused to meet the Indians at the foot of the bluff without an escort of soldiers and Captain Jack could see no reason for them coming with soldiers to make peace.

While this dickering was going on, there was almost daily communication between the two camps, and the Indians who came to military headquarters, carried back tales that didn't help the cause of peace in the least. Chief among these mischief makers were Bogus Charley and Boston Charley.

Bogus combined with his booming voice a smooth tongue unhindered by scruples. Even among his own tribe he was known as the "double-hearted man." Although his name came from Bogus Creek where he was born, he managed to live up to it very well, indeed. Able to sham any manner the situation demanded, he used all of his native cunning and shrewdness to take advantage of what he had learned from living with white men . . . . and unfortunately he had learned chiefly the worst elements of civilized life.

Boston Charley was hardly more than a boy, his sleepy-looking, expressionless eyes and weak mouth making him look half-witted, but he ran Bogus a close second in reputation for duplicity. He was not a full-blooded Modoc as Bogus was, his light complexion giving origin to his name. His tribesmen held a strange belief that he was a "natural born traitor," and as such, he could not be held responsible for his acts of deception,

saying of him that "he had two tongues in his mouth
. . . . one Indian and one white!"

So clever were these two young bucks in their false
pretenses that they had the soldiers and officers completely fooled. On their visits to headquarters, Bogus
and Boston were taken in and treated to whiskey and
good-natured banter, but they also acquired much
more than was intended for them.

Among these things was the belief that the feeling
toward the Modocs was dominated by a thirst for
vengeance. They were also led to believe by the
"squaw-men" that the great passion of the commissioners was to hang every redskin that they could get in
their power.

Thus Bogus and Boston returned to the Modoc
stronghold with fantastic tales, based on half-truths
and embellished by their own agile imaginations. All
this was going on behind the backs of the commissioners, of course, and then they wondered why the Modocs
were growing more and more stubborn and untractable.
They were left helpless to know how to proceed.

During this impasse, Esquire Steele of Yreka arrived
at Van Bremer's ranch at the invitation of the commissioners. Captain Jack had often asked to see Steele and
he looked like their one salvation. Perhaps this man,
who had formerly befriended the Modoc chief, might
be able to break the deadlock which existed. At least
the chances looked good if Steele was willing to risk
them.

When the situation was canvassed and the proposition put up to him, he consented to visit the enemy
stronghold and see what he could do. Accordingly,
armed with the authority to propose an amnesty for all
offenders, if they would consent to removal to some

distant reservation of their own choice, he prepared to
make the venture. The hitch in the plan was that the
Indians were to go to Angel Island in San Francisco
bay where they were to live as prisoners of war, fed and
clothed at government expense while plans for their
permanent home were being worked out.

Steele decided to take Frank Riddle and his wife,
Winema, as interpreters and John Fairchild as moral
support. William "Bill Dad" Atwood, newspaper reporter, stuffed his pockets full of paper and pencils,
pushed his high-crowned, broad brimmed hat to the
back of his head and prepared to go along without being
asked. Loaded with blankets and provisions for an over-
night stay, the party set out to call on the Modoc Chief.

Much to their surprise, the Modocs turned out to be
friendly . . . effusively so. Captain Jack called a council.
When all his braves had assembled, he made a long
speech . . . long, that is, for him. He explained again
that he was anxious for peace, stoutly declaring that
neither he nor his people had ever done anything to
warrant the treatment they had received.

Steele was sympathetic toward Jack's position and
told him that many others were also sympathetic. Then
he explained to them the new proposal, emphasizing
that the Great White Father had the best interests of his
children at heart and wanted them to enjoy a better life
in a home where they would be happy.

The response from the braves led Steele's party to
believe that the speech had been well-received and they
rolled up in their blankets that night well pleased with
the thought that they had been the means of solving the
Modoc trouble.

Next afternoon arrangements were made for several
of the Indians to accompany the white men back to

their camp. Everything went smoothly, and Steele, in his eagerness to spread the good news, rode on ahead of Fairchild and his Modoc escorts, and arrived at headquarters some time before his companions.

Even before he had reached the anxiously waiting group of commissioners, who were gathered to welcome him, he flung his hat in the air and shouted out the long-hoped-for words: "They accept peace!"

The apprehensive gloom that had pervaded the camp since his departure gave way to exultation. Couriers were dispatched to Yreka with glowing accounts for the Washington authorities and the press. Letters relating the good news were begun, preparations were started for a grand celebration, relief was manifest everywhere.

Then Fairchild arrived. He arrived with a different story than Steele's, which put a sudden check on all this exuberance. "I don't think the Modocs agreed to accept the terms offered," he said, gravely. "I admit they responded to Steele's speech, but not in the way he thought. I've just been talking to these Indians here, and I tell you they don't understand they've agreed to surrender on any terms!"

Steele was dumfounded. He turned to Bill Dad, sitting with his feet propped up on a camp table and asked him to read the speeches as he had taken them down. These, too, without question gave the impression that Steele's peace talk had been greeted with approval.

He sent for the Indians who had returned with his party and questioned them as to the understanding. They were now non-committal. "We come to listen, not to talk," they said. Not a thing could be learned from them.

In spite of that, Steele was so confident that he had

been successful in his peace efforts that he proposed to reassure himself and the commission by returning to Captain Jack's stronghold the next day. Fairchild, on being asked to go along, said nothing, but his narrowed eyes and the slow swinging of his head from side to side expressed plenty. Riddle, also, refused to return to the enemy camp, but was finally persuaded to allow Winema to go, since an interpreter was necessary.

So without Fairchild or Riddle, Steele, Bill Dad and Winema started back to check on their findings. By this time even they were haunted by a sense of foreboding that they tried to shake off in vain. They were left to make the journey alone, for the Indians who had accompanied them to headquarters had returned the night before, having seen all, heard all and said nothing.

The reception prepared for the white men made their hair stand on end. Here was no friendly tribe of Indians such as had greeted them before. The eyes that met those of Steele and his friends were darkly hostile. They were far more potent than words in convincing Steele that he had, indeed, been mistaken.

But although his long experience with Indians had not fully qualified him to understand them in council it had taught him that courage would command their respect where nothing else could. If he showed a yellow streak, he knew it would be the beginning of the end ... and that the beginning and the end would be all too close together!

He chose to ignore what he saw, and approached the Chief with outstretched hand, trying to appear indifferent to the ill-disguised animosity. Yet he was cautious. Only when Captain Jack gave Steele to understand that he was still his friend, did he feel in the least reassured.

Again the braves gathered in council. Their Chief's words told Steele nothing more than the actions of his men had already intimated. He said the Modocs had not yet shown their hearts, that his friend, Steele, had missed some of his words.

Steele replied that he had done them no intentional wrong; that he was their friend and wanted to remain so.

Schonchin John impetuously leapt to his feet "We are done talking peace!" he thundered at Steele, hatred in every gesture, every look. "We do not talk peace with men who betray us! You tell lies about us. You are like your brothers. We cannot trust them . . . none of them. Our hearts were not bad, but you made them bad with your lies. We will not make peace with the white man! We will fight for our Lost river country 'til every man of us is dead!"

Coolly, courageously, Steele faced Schonchin John before a battery of unfriendly eyes. His voice was steady, although in his heart, he knew that the man he faced intended to see that he would never have another opportunity to misrepresent the Modocs.

"I don't want to talk to a man when his heart is bad," he said simply. "When a man's heart is bad he says things he doesn't mean. We'll wait until tomorrow. Then we'll talk again."

Captain Jack rebuked Schonchin John and declared the council was at an end. Scattering about, the Modocs gathered in small groups, talking in low tones, and casting side-long glances at the white men.

Without saying in words that the braves led by Schonchin John had designs on their lives, Captain Jack and Scarface Charley prepared beds for the two

men and for Winema in the Chief's own cave. No
words were necessary for it was all too evident.

Several times during the fear-haunted hours that
followed, Steele looked from under his blankets and
saw the silent forms of Captain Jack, Scarface or Queen
Mary standing guard over him and his companions.
Well he knew that these self-appointed sentinels were
all that stood between them and death.

When the council reassembled next morning, angry
words and dark looks met Steele as before. Although
temporarily frustrated, the desire for murder was
obviously still there.

The situation called for strategy. As well try to reason with a volcano as to talk peace in such an atmosphere. The one thing Steele knew he could rely upon
was the good will of Captain Jack and his head man,
Scarface Charley. With no more to support him than
this, the best he could do was to propose that he would
return to headquarters and bring back with him all of
the commissioners.

After a heated argument, he was conceded permission
to depart only on those conditions . . . conditions that
he knew were equivalent to a promise that he would
lead his fellow peace-makers to the Modoc slaughter
pen.

Haggard, defeated, he arrived at the military camp
that night looking older by years than when he had
left the previous morning. He related what had happened in a straight-forward way, not attempting embel-
lishments nor self-justification. He had been mistaken.
He had escaped only on a promise that the commission
would visit the Lava Beds unarmed. Frankly, he declared that if they went, they would not come back
alive.

The Modocs were split into two factions, he said. The majority were desperate. The words, "Ben Wright" fell from their lips like a battle cry. They mistrusted all white men, and were out for revenge. If necessary they would resort to treachery themselves, and there was good reason to believe they thought it necessary.

CHAPTER IX

CRAFTY STRATEGEM

EVERY day now saw the addition of new recruits to the military forces surrounding the Lava Beds. The bayonets of the reinforcements glistened in the sunlight, their tramping feet broke the desert stillness that hung over this desolate country.

From all appearances the forces of war were gaining over those of peace. Members of the commission, discouraged with progress made or out of harmony with the government's policy, resigned almost as fast as they were appointed. Finally the personnel sifted down to Meacham who retained his position as chairman. General Canby who took time out from his other duties as Commander of the Department of the Columbia, to come to the scene of activities and supervise the work of the commission; L. S. Dyer, the elderly, but alert Indian agent for Klamath reservation, and Reverend Eleazar Thomas, a rotund, kindly clergyman from San Francisco.

The apparent failure of negotiations was emphasized, also, by General Gillem's decision to move the army nearer the stronghold of the enemy. He sent word to Captain Jack that he was doing so only to make it easier to communicate with him, and that they would not reopen hostilities unless the Modocs took the offensive.

On the last day of March, the camp at Van Bremer's ranch was broken up, and the next four days were spent in reestablishing it at the foot of the bluff close to the lake shore. Now the neat rows of white tents took on the appearance of a small village, so numerous had they become with the constant arrival of new troops.

On a jutting rock near the top of the cliff, a signal station was established. From there, with a field glass, the Modocs could be observed moving about in their rocky fortress not more than a mile and a half away. The site overlooked all of the country for miles and was ideal for the purpose of reconnoissance.

The next move was to set up direct contact with the detachment of soldiers at the sub-base on the opposite side of the stronghold. The three camps were almost in a direct line with each other and communication was possible by means of boats, although they had to pass in full view of the Modocs.

Shortly after the headquarters had been relocated, a new company of soldiers, moving up to join those already stationed in the Lava Beds, came upon about thirty Modoc ponies. With great gusto they captured them and proudly led their prizes into camp. Thereupon, the chairman of the peace commission and General Canby launched a dispute over whether or not this constituted a violation of the armistice which had been agreed upon. Meacham stubbornly insisted that it did, and that the stolen property should be returned immediately, whereas the general maintained that there

A. B. Meacham

"Medicine Rock" on the outskirts of Captain Jack's
stronghold

(Photo by Signal Corps, U. S. Army)

was no need of it . . . that they would be well-cared for and turned over when peace was made.

The Modocs were very fond of their horses and it was to be expected that they would protest, as they did. A small group of Indian women came to headquarters, asking for their ponies. They were refused. General Canby, however, permitted them to go under guard to the corrals.

They petted and stroked their horses which nuzzled against the women as if to welcome old friends. When the squaws were ordered to leave the corral, they turned away with wistful glances over their shoulders. The most encouragement they received was the promise they could have them when the Modocs had come to terms.

Other occasional visitors to the military encampment in the shadow of the bluff were a few of the Modoc braves who were permitted to mingle freely with the soldiers and civilians stationed there. This liberty was granted with the idea of impressing them with the friendly intentions of the peace commission and the power of the army. Everywhere they were confronted with the sight of arms and ammunition, howitzers and cannon balls, glittering brass buttons and bayonets.

The effect on the Indians was not altogether what the peace commission desired. They learned that General Gillem expected a hundred Warm Spring Indians to arrive soon . . . a tribe from a reservation far to the north, and one with whom the Modocs had always been on hostile terms. They resented, also, the signal telegraph, the workings of which they couldn't understand.

Very perturbed, Bogus Charley and Hooker Jim questioned General Gillem about these things. "What for you talk over my home?" Bogus demanded. "Me no like that. What for Warm Springs come here? What for you bring so many soldiers to make peace?"

The general, who more than matched Bogus' and Hookers' six feet in height, seemed to look down on his questioners from an even greater elevation, his dignity bolstered by the impressiveness of his uniform and enhanced by beard and side whiskers. His reply was condescending. We are doing all these things for your own good," he said and then warned, "And don't you dare to shoot my men. I won't shoot your men unless you shoot first!"

Fear took possession of the Modocs, but not so much fear of power as renewed fear of treachery. Although they were no match for the white men in numbers and equipment, they knew if treachery was in the wind they could do their share . . . and possibly do it first.

This skepticism of the soldiers' motives was in large part responsible for the failure of several attempts made since Steele's visit to bring the Modocs to terms. After the last unsuccessful effort was reported to Washington, D. C., the commission received the following reply:

"Continue negotiations. But should these peaceful measures fail and should the Modocs presume so far upon the forbearance of the government and again resort to deceit and treachery, I trust you will make such use of the military force that no other Indian tribe will imitate their example and that no reservation will be needed for them except graves among their chosen Lava Beds."

The outlook for positive results was most discouraging, since the only outcome of the previous meetings had been an agreement between the hostile factions that a tent should be erected mid-way between the two camps so that the peace negotiations could be carried on. This was prompted by the deluge of rain in which the last conference had taken place, sudden storms being very common in this locality.

On the fifth of April, Captain Jack sent Boston Charley, requesting "old man Meacham" to meet him at this council tent and to bring Fairchild along. Although the commissioners were fearful of consequences, knowing as they did the growing antagonism among the fractious members of the band, they were under orders from Washington to make full speed ahead. Under this pressure, Meacham and Fairchild agreed to take the chance, Frank and Winema Riddle going along as interpreters.

When they arrived at the tent, they found Captain Jack and seven or eight braves awaiting them. The Chief expressed himself as being very pleased that they had come alone. He said he was afraid of General Canby with his fancy uniform and of Reverend Thomas because he was a "Sunday Doctor". All this was interpreted into English by Winema, who continued to act as a go-between for what followed.

"But now I can talk freely," Jack said, stanced with feet apart and arms folded. "I am not afraid now. I know your hearts. You take away the soldiers and the war will stop. Give me and my people a home on Lost river. I can take care of them. I do not need government's help. We don't want to ask an agent where we can go and what we can do. We are *men!* We are not women!"

Meacham interrupted the loading of his pipe and shook his head. "Since blood has been spilled on Lost river you could not live there in peace. The blood would always come between you and the white men.

The army can't be taken away until all the trouble is settled."

Captain Jack sat on a rock and remained silent for a moment. When he spoke it was regretfully, sadly. "I hear your words. I will give up my home on Lost river. You give me these Lava Beds for a home. My people can live good here. You don't want these rocks. They no good to white man."

Meacham and Fairchild sat down, too. "No, Jack, we can't do that," Meacham said. "The only way we can make peace is for you to consent to leave the country entirely or at least give up for trial the men who murdered the settlers on the shores of Tule lake."

"Who will try them? White men or Indians?"

"White men, of course."

"Then will you give up your men who killed our women and children on Lost river for Indian trial?"

"No, that would be impossible. The Modoc law is dead. The white men rule the country now. Only one law can live at a time."

Captain Jack took another tack. "Then will you try the white men, who killed my people, by white man's law?"

Meacham would have liked to say "yes" to this proposal, but he knew it couldn't be done. The prejudice against the Indians was too strong. He could only reply, "That wouldn't do you or your people any good, Jack. The Indian law is dead."

Bitterness hardened Captain Jack's features. "So that is how it is! White man's laws are made for white man. They leave Indian out!" he retorted. "No, I cannot give up my young men to be hanged. I know they did wrong. Their blood was bad when they saw their women and children dead. I can't help that. I have no strong laws or jail houses like you do. Your men are bad, too. Why don't you make your own men do right?"

Meacham realized there was no answer to that, so he ignored the question. "If you refuse to give them up then you must come out of the rocks with all your people. That is the only way we can make peace. We will hunt up a new home for you where there will be no more trouble."

"We don't want any other country! The Great Spirit put my people there first. I was born there. My father was born there. I don't want a home anywhere else."

"But you can't live there any longer, Jack," Meacham repeated. "The settlers would never let you live there in peace after all that has happened."

The Chief's reply was caustic. "You say to come out of the rocks. You say we must put ourselves in your power. I say no! When we started out talking peace you said, 'Jack, promise you won't prepare for more fighting until everything is settled . . . . until the peace-making is over. If you promise, we will do the same.' I said, 'All right. Jack's word is good and solid like a big rock. I won't get ready to fight any more until peace-talks are over.'

"I kept my promise. When your men came through the country I could have killed them. I did not. My men stayed in the rocks. They didn't kill any cattle or steal any horses. My word is good like I said. But yours is weak like water. You are all liars. Your soldiers took my horses. They wouldn't give them back. You say you want to make more peace. How come you bring so many soldiers to make peace? Every day your men come with big guns. Guns for making war not peace!"

He turned with a sweeping gesture, pointing to the far shore of Tule lake. "You see that dark spot? The Modocs met Ben Wright there. I was a little boy then, but I remember. He said he was friend of Modocs. He invited us to a peace feast. It was raining hard. My people wore moccasins. Their feet were wet. They sat down by the fire to dry them.

"Ben Wright, he smoked the pipe with them. They thought he was a good man. They believed him. Then they discovered he put poison in the food. They would not eat. Wright he get mad, draw pistol and shoot my father dead. His men, they shoot my defenseless people. Do you know how many escaped? Do you know?"

With his eyes fixed fiercely on Meacham, he raised one hand with five fingers extended in silent answer.

Meacham nodded and pointed to Bloody Point. "And do you remember how many escaped there?"

"We were not talking peace then," the chief replied quickly. "We had not smoked the pipe."

"It is true that Ben Wright did wrong to fire under a pretense of peace-making, but . . . ."

Jack interrupted tersely. "You say Ben Wright did wrong. Your government didn't say he was a bad man. Great White Father made him ty-ee chief . . . . made him Indian agent!"

When Meacham failed to reply, Captain Jack, Kientepoos, Chief of the Modocs, rose to his full stature and beat himself on the chest with his fist.

"I am but one man. I am the voice of the Modocs. What their hearts say, that I do. I want no more war. But I want to be treated like a man! I may have red skin but my heart is white. If you refuse to treat me like a man, I will die with my enemies beneath me. I will not fall on the sharp rocks!

"Your soldiers began on me when I was asleep at Lost river. They chased me to the rocks like a wounded deer. Tell your soldier ty-ee that I am waiting for him here. Tell him not to look for me on Lost river or Shasta Butte. Tell him I am here. I am not afraid to die! I will show him how a Modoc can die!"

"You will regret this, Jack," Meacham warned. "If you refuse to come out of the rocks you must face the consequences. And remember. Not only you but all your people will be destroyed!"

When Meacham left that conference it was with more respect for the Modoc Chief than he had ever felt before. It was the first . . . . and the last . . . . full, free talk that was had with Captain Jack during the existence of the commission.

Reports of the meeting spread rapidly among the Modocs and that night many of the braves gathered around the camp fire in council while Captain Jack remained secluded in his own cave. In his absence, free rein was given to the more fractious element of the band.

Feeling in favor of assassinating the commissioners ran high. Schonchin John, inflamed with a deep seated jealousy of Captain Jack, based on his desire to become Chief, brought the question to a head. He jumped to his feet and said heatedly, "Many times Modocs trapped and fooled by white man's words! These peace mans, they try to fool us now. They keep on talking peace so more and more soldiers can come. When all here, then they kill Modocs easy like shooting geese!"

Other leaders of the mutinous faction followed

Schonchin John's lead, haranguing their tribesmen with the necessity for making the first move against the white men, and making it soon. After several Indians had spoken, a handsome young brave rose quietly from where he was sitting some distance from the sagebrush fire. It was William Faithful. He walked to the center of the semi-circle of braves and stood on the windward side of the flames where the smoke wouldn't choke his words.

"Me no think Schonchin and you others see straight," he began. "Schonchin, him not our head Chief. Captain Jack is Chief of the Modocs. We do wrong to make plot against white men when him not here. Let us send for Jack and hear his words."

Reluctantly the others consented and a man was dispatched to summon their Chief from his cave where he had been unaware of what was going on. When he appeared, William Faithful told him what they wanted. He said they wanted to know his conclusions after his peace talk with the commissioners . . . that he must weigh his words carefully, since he, William, would stand by his judgment.

The light from the fire was dim and flickering at best, and Jack found it hard to see the men before him. Yet he sensed that something was wrong. There was an undercurrent of feeling that seemed to charge the very air. The chief stood silent, searching their faces with his keen eyes. When he spoke, it was slowly, as if each word was of great importance.

"My people, your Chief knows you are restless. It takes long time to make peace. It is not easy, but it is better than fighting. But if we do not lose heart, we will get what we want. Maybe not Lost river. Maybe we go to Yainax. The rest of our people live there in peace. Why can't we?"

At this Schonchin John flared up anew. "Yes, me have brother at Yainax. He live there in peace. But he no kill white man. We have. They never let us live there in peace!"

"I think we could," Jack insisted. "I do this way with peace-makers. I hold out for home at Hot Creek or Lava Beds. They see I no give up, they offer us Yainax. I say 'Yes, I go with all my people if you forget past and not make my men be tried by white man's law for murder.' You stick to Jack, he pull you out all right. You see!"

Black Jim, a morose, shifty-eyed brave, who had previously held himself aloof from the feud between the Chief and Schonchin John, now definitely aligned himself with the latter. "Jack, you never save your people that way. More soldiers come every two, three days. Bring big guns. Shoot bullets big as man's head. Those pow-wow mans make peace by blowing off heads of Modocs! Only one way we must do. We must kill white man first. Long time ago before so many soldiers come, we should have killed them! If we must die, better die now!"

"My people," Jack countered. "Your talk, maybe, seem good to you. But my way is better and safer for all of us."

In their excitement the braves pushed closer to him, each trying to be heard above the other. "No! Your talk no good!" they cried. "We like Black Jim's words. We have to die anyway, let us fight so we die like men, not sick ducks!"

The Chief turned from his war-crazed people. "Your

blood is hot like fire! Let us talk no more until it is
cool."

Schonchin John blocked his way. "You say you are
head Chief. Promise, you kill soldier ty-ee!"

"No! Canby good man. Him friend of Modocs.
Jack no kill him!" At the threatening words and actions
of his men the Chief became alarmed, but he maintained a calm front. "You no play fair! You want to
force me to act like coward!" he protested.

"No, no! We ask you to act like brave man! You
no kill him, then you coward. You kill Canby, white
men know Captain Jack is brave Indian. Him true
Modoc!"

"But it is wrong to kill soldier-ty-ee while having
peace-talk. No! I will not promise to kill him!"

"You no kill, huh? Yes, you will!" one of his men
taunted, catching up a basket from one of the squaws
and placing it on the Chief's head. Another threw a
woman's shawl over his shoulders. "Chief, him no-
good coward!" they hooted. "Him bird-hearted
squaw!"

Stung by the words of derision, Jack made an attempt to escape from his tormentors. One of the braves
tripped him, and others pushed him back against the
rocks. "You have heart like fish!" they mocked. "You
no Modoc! White man, him steal your heart!"

Angered beyond endurance by these accusations,
Jack struggled to his feet, dashing aside the hat and
shawl. "You liars!" he shouted, letting his voice rise
above the clamor around him. "You liars! Jack him
true Modoc. Him Chief of Modocs! Me no white-
faced squaw! You say kill white men, all right. We
kill them! But hear Jack's words! No Modoc live to

tell of this day! Maybe we kill few white men, but white men kill every Modoc!"

Fiercely he pushed the braves from his path and went to his cave. From where he sat with his head in his hands, he could hear the exultant shouts of Schonchin John and the other warriors as they celebrated the victory over their Chief with a war-dance far into the night.

For two days Jack stayed in his cave, refusing to see or talk to anyone. Over and over in his mind he turned the problem of how to get his men to release him from the rash promise he had made in the heat of anger. At last he sent for William Faithful and asked him to call all of the braves into council. "Jack want to have council in daytime so he can look his people in the face when he make talk," he told William.

From cave to cave William went, telling the people that their Chief wanted them all to gather at an appointed time. Every warrior agreed to be there.

At the time set, the sun broke through the clouds that had brought long-continued stormy weather and the braves gathered in the first sunshine they had known for days. When they had all seated themselves on rocks and brush, Captain Jack came from his cave and strode back and forth several times before his braves. No word was spoken among the men who were tensely awaiting the words of their Chief.

At last Jack stopped, folded his arms across his chest. His firm, piercing gaze fell on first one man and then another. Many stared at the ground, unable to look him in the eye, but others met his gaze with a look as defiant as his own. When he spoke it was with the determination of a man who has made up his mind. "My people, I feel ashamed. I feel as if I was lost among a strange people. My heart tells me I might as well talk to the clouds and the wind. But I must speak!"

Undaunted by their obvious antagonism, he brought out argument after argument in an effort to make them see things as he saw them . . . the hopelessness of defying the white men . . . the folly of committing treachery.

"My people," he concluded, "You made me promise to kill Canby. Do not hold me to that promise. I was angry when I said I would kill him. If you hold me to the promise I made when my blood was hot, we are all doomed!"

Hooker Jim, one of those who had met the Chief's gaze with defiance, rose and stood before him.

"You talk good, but too late for such talk. We say you must keep your words! You must kill Canby!" The words rang out like an ultimatum.

Jack sent a look of appeal to the other men of the tribe. "I can't believe that you all want me to kill the soldier-ty-ee. Those who want me to do this coward's deed, stand on their feet!"

To his dismay, all except about a dozen, rose. Again he put the question. "Shall I kill the white man chief?"

"Yes, kill him!"

"Remember Ben Wright!"

"Yes, we say yes!"

The answer came from many lips.

"All right, I will keep my word. But my people, if Canby refuse us a home in our country, I will ask him many times. If he says yes, I will not kill him. Only, if he won't agree to give us what we want . . . only, then will I kill him! Do you hear? Only, then will I kill Canby!"

They growled their assent and Captain Jack asked if that would satisfy them.

"Yes, him no give us what we want, you kill him then," Hooker Jim conceded. "That all right."

This implied, of course, the assassination of the rest of the commissioners. The method to be used was hotly debated among the warriors. Some thought they ought to be shot down from ambush. Others maintained that they should be lured into another peace-talk and killed in cold blood as Ben Wright had treated their people twenty years before. The conditions which Captain Jack had wrung from them finally swung the vote in favor of massacre at a peace-talk.

The braves wrangled about who should do the killing. They finally decided to choose their victims in the order of the tribal rank of the men who were to participate in the massacre. General Canby, of course, fell to the Chief, who selected Ellen's Man as his assistant.

Schonchin John spoke for "old man Meacham", and chose Shacknasty Jim to help dispose of him. Reverend Thomas, the "Sunday Doctor", was assigned to Boston and Bogus Charley, who had each received a new suit of clothes from him the day before. To Hooker Jim and Black Jim fell the "honor" of dispatching Mr. Dyer.

Next came Frank and Winema Riddle. Before their fate had been decided, Scarface Charley jumped to his feet. "Riddle and Winema, they our friend. Me no see them killed! Who kills them dies from Scarface Charley's gun. I have spoken!"

Every Modoc warrior knew Scarface would do as he threatened and no one ventured to assume the responsibility for killing the white man and his squaw wife.

Curly Head Doctor, eager for glory as always, had

planned a massacre of his own on a smaller scale. The medicine man and Curly Jack announced that they would decoy Colonel Mason from his camp at the southeastern tip of the lake and dispose of him, too.

The plans were complete and all that remained was to set their trap and lure the commissioners into it.

CHAPTER X

"SHOOT ME IF YOU DARE"

AFTER the talk Meacham and Fairchild had with Captain Jack in the Lava Beds, they returned to camp and went into conference with General Canby, Reverend Thomas and Dyer. Both men declared themselves convinced that Captain Jack honestly desired peace; that he was willing to accept the terms offered. It was Curly Head Doctor, Schonchin John and their bloodthirsty fellows who were causing all the trouble. They had tied their Chief's hands.

Meacham had concluded his account of the meeting with the Modocs by saying, "Their Chief is overruled by the majority of the tribe who have faith in Curly Head Doctor's medicine making. With his 'magic' on their side, they actually believe they could whip our forces, strong as we are."

"But if Captain Jack is willing to give up his claim to Lost river, that's a big step," General Canby pointed out, as he thoughtfully chewed on his stub of a cigar. "He's always, heretofore, refused flatly. If we press him further, don't you suppose we can get him to consent to the removal? We don't want to give up just as we're within sight of success."

"Not a chance in the world!" Fairchild insisted. "His people won't let him. The trouble with Jack is that he's too weak to act without their approval and too strong to give in to 'em."

Reverend Thomas, his nearly-bald head glistening in the sun, offered a compromise as a solution. "Well, it seems a shame to make him, and others who favor peace, suffer because some of the tribal members carry the devil in their hearts," he said, gravely. "Why couldn't we send a message to Captain Jack, stating that if he and the peace party will come out, we'll protect them with the troops while they're doing it? Then we could deal with the Indians who want to fight in accordance with what they deserve."

Others hailed this suggestion as a possible way out of their dilemma . . . all except John Fairchild who looked up at the sky with a dubious expression. "It's a good idea, all right, but it won't work," he asserted, bluntly.

"Nevertheless, it might be worth trying," Canby said. "But perhaps we'd better wait for a day or two for developments and see what reaction there is in the Modoc camp. Who knows? They may take the initiative and accept the terms already offered, after they've thought it over." The others agreed.

Among the army men in the military encampment, opinion on the situation was as diversified as the men themselves and, besides, there was plenty of time for airing of views during the forced idleness of waiting.

Later in the day the men chief in command of the army, which now numbered close to a thousand, were sitting about on camp stools and cots in General Gillem's tent.

"Well, General," Gillem remarked, "Whenever you're through trying to make peace with those fellows, I think I can bring them in without the loss of more than a half dozen men."

Canby said nothing and Gillem continued, "Oh, we'd have some casualties, of course, in wounded men; but you just give the order and I'll see that we get them out of there."

For a moment no one spoke. General Canby shifted the cigar in his mouth and fixed his eyes on Colonel Mason with a questioning look. The colonel, who had been transferred to the other camp and who had just arrived by boat with Colonel Barnard for a short visit at headquarters, seemed to understand the thought that Canby didn't care to put into words.

He nodded toward Gillem and said, "With due deference to the opinion of General Gillem, I think that if we take them out with the loss of a third of our entire command we'll be doing as well as I expect."

Colonel Barnard's portly form swayed back and forth as much as to say, "I agree with you, Colonel."

The tent flap opened and Colonel John Green stepped in.

"Good. I'm glad you came," Canby greeted him. "I'd like to know, Colonel, what *you* think about our chances. How many men would you say it would cost us to bring the Modocs out of the rocks?"

"I don't know," Green replied, evasively. "Only, I do know on the seventeenth, we got licked like the very devil!"

Canby nodded and continued to chew on the cigar which had long since ceased to have fire in it. No doubt, the opinions of these men made a deep impression on the commanding general. Gillem had successfully fought rebels in Tennessee. The other three men had fought rebels successfully in the Civil war, too, but they had, also, fought rebels *unsuccessfully* in the Lava Beds. Naturally, he credited their opinions more than Gillem's.

In a tent a hundred yards away, another discussion was going on. These were the younger officers, having a "bull session" in which the peace commission came in for a verbal trouncing. These men had their stripes to win on the field of battle. They were brave, ambitious. Bitterly they complained that the peace commission had no right to subject an army of hundreds to the humiliation of waiting in idleness while four or five men tried to talk peace into Captain Jack. The only talk those redskins understood was the language of lead and bayonets. Just let a bunch of regulars get at them, when they weren't soused in fog, and they'd whip them to a standstill!

Colonel Green, passing by on his way from the conference he had just left, overheard the heated words of impatience and denunciation. He stepped to the tent opening. The men rose to salute. When he spoke he made no attempt to conceal the disapproval in his voice.

"Stop that talk," he said. "The peace commission have as much right here as we have. They're the best friends we have. God grant them success. I've been in the Lava Beds once, and if the memories of some of you aren't too short, you won't abuse the peace commission, gentlemen!"

The fiery young officers respected the man who spoke. They said no more.

In the commissioners' tent a little farther down the line, three of the peace-makers were assembled. Grave, thoughtful, the dignified Reverend Thomas sat on a camp chair near the stove. Dyer sat humped on a box, his elbows on his knees, his chin in his hands. Meacham moved about replenishing the stove with sagebrush. There was a rap on the tent pole.

"Come in," Meacham called.

A fine looking, middle-aged officer entered. After the usual compliments were passed, he announced that he was out for a good growl and that they seemed to be as good victims as any.

"Growl away," Meacham invited.

"Well, why don't you pull out and give us a chance at those Modocs? If you don't we'll be lying around here all spring and summer without even a crack at them! We hate all this fooling around, but there's no convincing General Canby. You know you can't make any headway with that bunch of double-crossers. They're just stalling off and you know it. How about giving the army a chance to clean 'em out and be done with it?"

Meacham, who agreed with Mason, Barnard and Green on the terrible loss of life such a course would involve, asked Wright if he thought it would be worth all it cost.

"Hell, it's costing plenty as it is . . . . not in lives, maybe, but in greenbacks. And what's more, it'll all boil down to a scrap in the end, anyway. You mark my words!" Wright asserted.

"Maybe it will, and maybe it won't," Meacham replied. "But at least we'll feel we've done everything we can to save the best part of several hundred men from rotting in the Lava Beds!"

"The trouble with you is they've got you scared . . . you and Canby and all the rest. Why, I'll bet you two thousand dollars that Lieutenant Eagan's company and mine can whip the Modocs in fifteen minutes once we get in position. And if you don't think I mean it, I'll put the money on the line!"

"Well, my dear Wright, you might make out a petition to General Canby asking him to send the rest of the army home right away while you and Eagan perform the heroics. As things stand, I guess you know that Canby isn't willing to move on the Modocs until the Warm Spring Indians arrive. I'll admit I agree with you on one thing and that is the prospects of making peace with them. I wouldn't be surprised that you'll get the chance to have it out with the big Chief, but I'd advise you to hang onto your two thousand dollars, and keep the rest of the army handy when you get ready to do it."

Lieutenant Wright, somewhat appeased, soon left saying that he felt better now that he'd gotten his "growl off his chest."

There had been a noticeable increase in desertions the past few days, as word had passed around that there was little hope of making peace with the Modocs. Now that action seemed imminent, many of the boys who had nothing but scars to win on the field of battle, decided to seek a climate more conducive to long life. Those who had met the Modocs once had no desire to do so again and their reports had demoralized many of the newcomers.

Among others, the man who had been employed as cook for the peace commissioners had departed for parts unknown. That left them to do their own rustling and the next morning found Meacham and Dyer preparing breakfast of cornbread and coffee when a couple of soldiers joined them.

"I say, cap'n, have you give up tryin' to make peace with them Injuns?" one of them began.

"Don't know for sure, why?" Meacham replied.

"Well, 'cause why them boys as has been in there, says as how it's sure lightnin'. Them Modocs don't give a feller a chance. I'm tellin' ya, we don't want no Modoc!"

"Yes, I know," Meacham agreed. "It'll be tough on you boys. But if the plan we have in mind now doesn't work out, it begins to look like you'd have to go and bring them in."

The other soldier who had been squatting beside the stove rose and said, "Mr. Commissioner, we want you to know us boys is all your friends. We was sure hopin' you'd get 'em to come around. Are you certain there ain't nothin' for it but fightin' 'em?"

"Just one chance and it doesn't look too good. We're about at the end of our rope, and I'm afraid it's going to be up to you fellows to do the rest." Meacham started to pour the coffee. "Have some?" he invited.

"No thank you," they mumbled and disconsolately returned to their quarters to tell their comrades what they had gleaned from the conversation.

After waiting several days for the Modocs to make the next move, it became apparent that there was no hope of that, so the peace commissioners determined to try out the plan suggested by Reverend Thomas, of bringing in those who desired peace. Winema was summoned, instructed just what to say, then dispatched to the Modoc stronghold with the proposition. She mounted her pony and set out over the trail which by now had been sufficiently cleared of rocks so that a horse could travel it with only slight difficulty.

On her arrival, she sought Captain Jack and tried to

talk with him alone, but when he learned she had news from the commission, he told her, "I want all my people to hear," and immediately called them into council.

The proposition that those who desired peace would come out under protection of the troops, was put before the Modocs and a vote taken. Only eleven men lined up with Captain Jack, agreeing to accept the terms. The rest ... thirty-eight of them ... not only voted against it, but issued a sinister warning that no Modoc would ever give himself up alive.

Captain Jack turned to Winema, who had been watching the voting procedure hopefully, yet fearfully. "I am Chief of the Modocs," he said. "Tell the soldier-ty-ee and old man Meacham, Captain Jack will not desert his people. Tell them we will fight for our homes. But we will not fire the first shot. Tell them that!"

Anxious for the safety of her kinsmen and disappointed at what she had seen and heard,Winema started back through the rocks with the discouraging news. Suddenly she heard a hissing noise. She stopped, peering apprehensively on all sides. She could see nothing. But as she started to move on, she heard a hoarse whisper from behind a rock, speaking her native tongue, the language of the Modocs.

"You no stop!" it said. "You stop, they see me, they kill me. Me warn you, tell old man Meacham and peace men they no more come to council tent! They get killed!"

Winema caught a brief glimpse of her friend, William Faithful. She wanted to ask him more, but he slipped silently away. Tense with apprehension, she spurred her horse on, causing it to stumble over the rough trail. Her distress was obvious to those waiting for her at headquarters, but she refused to speak to anyone but her husband, Frank Riddle. She sat on her horse in silence until he had been summoned. On hearing her story, he drew Meacham away from the others and told him, with whitened lips, of the intended treachery.

"But why should they resort to anything like that?" Meacham asked, incredulously. "Surely they know it would bring the whole army down upon them! It's that devil, Curly Head Doctor . . . !"

His first thought was to call the rest of the commission aside and tell them the news. He was about to do so when Riddle grasped his arm. "No, don't do that!" His words were staccato, his eyes fearful. "Meacham, we've known you a long time. We trust you. But these other men. How do we know they won't tell who told them? The Modocs would kill Tobey if they found out she betrayed them!"

"Never fear, Frank," Meacham reassured him. "You can bank on me and I'll see that the others promise to tell no one. We wouldn't endanger your lives for anything after the way you've helped us."

General Canby, Reverend Thomas, Dyer and Fairchild were summoned to Riddle's tent. Each pledged himself to absolute secrecy. General Canby was the first to do so, turning to Winema with the words, "Mrs. Riddle, I promise I'll never say a word to anyone of what you tell us. You can depend on me."

Reverend Thomas said, "Sister Tobey, I'm a minister of the gospel. I have my God to meet, and in the name of Christ, I promise I'll never divulge any secret you have to tell us." Dyer and Fairchild each assured her, also, that she could trust them.

After relating what she had heard, Winema exhorted

them to heed the warning. "What I tell you is the truth. Do not meet them in council again, for they plan to kill you and what they plan they will do. I know them!"

General Canby smiled, emphasizing the prominent crows' feet about his eyes. To him it all seemed a little absurd. "But they wouldn't dare to do that!" he exclaimed. "Why, that little handful of Modocs would be crazy to defy an army of hundreds!"

Reverend Thomas appeared unperturbed. "I trust in God to protect us," he said, piously. "God would never let them do such a wicked thing!"

Riddle was impatient with such sentiments and said so. "Gentlemen, I've known these Modocs for years. They may be crazy, but if they've decided to kill you, they'll do it in spite of heaven and all the angels! I know they'll do it!" Meacham, Dyer and Fairchild agreed with him. There was nothing that could be done about it that night, however, so they decided to wait to see what the morning would bring.

As things turned out, it brought a delegation of Indians composed of Bogus, Boston Charley and Shacknasty Jim, proposing a meeting at the council tent. They told Meacham, who was in charge of arranging for the councils, that Captain Jack and four other Indians were waiting at the peace tent for the commissioners to meet them.

While this parley was going on, an orderly approached the group and handed General Canby a dispatch from the signal station. He read it and without a change in expression on his clean shaven face, passed it on to Meacham. "Five Indians at council tent, apparently armed and about twenty more with rifles secreted in the rocks a few rods behind them," it read. Careful not to evince the least distrust, Meacham turned to Boston Charley and told him they weren't ready to talk yet.

Boston Charley was visibly disappointed and launched into a heated argument, trying every inducement he knew to get the commissioners to meet with Jack that day. But he succeeded only in convincing them, by the very heat of his words, that treachery was, indeed, intended.

Just as the three disgruntled Modocs were about to return to Captain Jack without their prey, Reverend Thomas approached Bogus Charley, putting his hands on Bogus' shoulders as if to give him blessing. "Bogus," he said, hoping to come to a better understanding of the Modocs' intentions, "Bogus, what do you want to kill us for? You know we're your friends. The Great White Father sent us here to make peace with you and take you to a good country."

Immediately Bogus' suave manner changed to one of suspicion and alarm. "Who tell you that?" he demanded. "Who tell you we want to kill peace mans?"

Thomas evaded. Bogus insisted. Each time Thomas refused to tell, Bogus grew more determined to find out. He towered over the clergyman with a threat in his movements that was enough to throw fear into any man. But although Thomas was thoroughly shaken, it was probably not that which caused him to weaken. More likely, this minister of the gospel was simply too honest to evade indefinitely; at any rate, he finally gave in. "Tobey told it," he admitted.

"This woman lies!" Bogus declared savagely.

"I thought there was no basis for alarm," Thomas breathed with relief.

Bogus signaled to Boston Charley and Shacknasty, and after a brief whispered consultation, the two started on a trot for the council tent and Captain Jack. Then Bogus, the "double-hearted man", walked back to where Thomas was standing and assured him that everything was all right. Arm in arm, the two men strolled over to Meacham's tent where they found the rest of the commissioners assembled, as well as Riddle and Winema.

Bogus expanded into unusual friendliness, reiterating that it was too bad they couldn't have a meeting that day, for he felt sure terms could be agreed upon. "Modocs, we very tired living in rocks. We ready make peace quick," he said. With such talk he held the attention of the commissioners while his fellows were speeding to their Chief on swift feet with word that Winema had betrayed them.

Soon Hooker Jim's evil-looking face and stooped shoulders appeared through the tent flap. "Cap'n Jack, him want to see Winema. Him want her to come to his cave," he announced, unceremoniously.

"Wants to see me?" Winema questioned in surprise. Followed by Meacham and her husband, she stepped out of the tent.

"What does Captain Jack want with Tobey?" Meacham demanded of Hooker.

"Him want to know why she tell lies about us Modocs!"

"Tells lies? What makes him think that?"

"We know she tell lie. She tell you we kill peace mans next time they come to council tent."

"Who said she told us such a thing?"

"Sunday Doctor, him told us. Him you call 'God's man'."

Just then Reverend Thomas joined them. "What's

this, my friends? You must be troubled to look so serious!"

Jaws set, eyes flashing, Riddle looked Thomas straight in the eye. "Thomas, you lied, you double-crossing sky-pilot! You promised my wife you'd keep her secret, and this is how you do it! Now Captain Jack's sent for her. Listen to me, Thomas! If anything happens to Tobey, because of this, I'll shoot you down like a skulking coyote!"

Thomas threw up his hands in dismay. "But you don't understand, Brother Riddle. I thought I was acting for the best. I was forced into it. You should get down on your knees and pray Almighty God to forgive you for what you've just said!"

"Pray! You're the one who should pray! But you could pray the caps off your knees and God would never forgive what *you've* done!"

Thomas shrunk back in hurt amazement and Riddle whirled on his heel as if the very sight of the man were poison to him.

"You come," Hooker was urging Winema. "Jack, he say me no come back without you."

"I'll go," Winema replied huskily, a pallor showing beneath her dusky skin.

Frank pleaded with her not to risk her life by going while Jack was still infuriated. "Wait a while, at least," he begged. "There's no telling what Jack might do when he's mad! He might even kill you!"

Winema shook her head slowly and asked him to bring her horse. He saw that she had made up her mind and he knew better than to try to change it, for she was as stubborn in her way as Jack was in his. Grimly he strode toward the corral.

While he was gone, Meacham did his best to dissuade

her. "But I don't think you should go," he insisted.
"It's too dangerous. Let him come here if he wants to
see you!"

"No, I must go." Winema's words were steady,
although the hand that rested lightly on her twelve-
year-old son's head was trembling. "I must go. I am
not afraid!"

Canby put his hand on her shoulder. "Tobey," he
said, his lower lip quivering a little as it always did
under the stress of emotion. "Tobey, if you insist on going, I'll promise you this. If Captain Jack threatens you,
I'll move in on him with my whole army!"

"I am not afraid," Winema repeated. "I have tried
to do all I can to make peace. I will not stop now."

Her husband came back with the pony, which she
had ridden on so many perilous errands, all saddled
and bridled. He started to help her mount. Her small
son stood gazing at her, his eyes brimming with tears
which he tried bravely to hold back. She left the horse,
to run and clasp him in her arms, stroking his hair and
pressing him to her. He began to cry and she squatted
on the ground, drawing him down onto her lap, drying
his tears, as choking sobs came from her lips.

The men looked on in embarrassed silence, scarcely
able to control their feelings. At last she regained her
self-control, and standing the lad on his feet, told him
to be a brave boy, reassuring him that she would return
soon.

Brushing the tears from her eyes with the back of her
hand, she moved toward her horse which was impatiently stamping the ground. Her husband helped her to
mount. There were a few almost inaudible spoken
words between them. Then, with a wave of her hand to
the others, she rode off, not allowing herself so much as

a glance at the lad who had tugged at her skirts and still called to her, until Riddle took him by the arm and led him back to their tent.

Thus did Winema set out to meet her own people . . . the people she had betrayed to the white men.

When she reached Jack's stronghold, it was like facing a barrage of bullets, so fierce and full of hatred were the looks she received from the braves who had gathered to await her coming. She dismounted slowly and cautiously, keeping a firm hand on the halter as the Indians gathered around her. With angry tones and accusing words, several braves started talking all at once, demanding to know by what authority she had told the white men of their intention to kill them.

Captain Jack motioned them back. In sullen silence, they watched their Chief as he stood before Winema, his arms crossed on his chest, his eyes smoldering with anger.

"Why for you tell white man we kill them?" he challenged. "You no Modoc woman! You white-hearted squaw-woman. How you know you tell white man true words? Who tell you?"

"Then it is true!" Winema countered. "You do intend to kill them!"

"Me no say it is true. Me want to know who tell you lies to tell white man!"

"Nobody has to tell me what I know is true. I know you plan to kill them because I . . . . I dreamed it!"

"No! You no dream it. One of my men, he tell you. You no tell who betray us, my men they kill you!"

"Well, it is true I did not dream it. The spirits told me. Spirits, they never lie."

"Spirits never tell you Jack plans to kill peace men!

You tell me who told you, my men they kill him. You no say quick, my men they kill you!"

At his words, a half-dozen braves leveled their guns at Winema, their fingers upon the triggers. She hesitated an instant before the determined look on their faces . . . but only an instant. Jumping onto a rock, with clenched fist Winema beat her breast.

"Shoot me, then, you cowards!" she cried in a loud voice. "I did not dream it. The spirits did not tell me. One of your own men told me! He is standing before me now. But do you think I will tell you who he is? No! Maybe I am a white man's woman, but I am a Modoc. All my blood is Modoc. My heart is brave. Braver than all you cowards who would kill a woman! Go ahead and shoot! My secret dies with me. Shoot, I say! Shoot me if you dare!"

She flung open her coat and stood there . . . . stood waiting for death, her head held high.

For the time it would take a snake to coil and strike, she stood there . . . . waiting. Then her eyes dropped to the silent warriors before her. She no longer stared into the muzzles of guns. They were being slowly lowered as a look of reluctant admiration displaced the fierce glances which she had encountered, but a moment before.

Captain Jack held up his hand. "Put away your guns!" he commanded. "This woman speaks brave words. Her heart is brave and strong like a big rock. She is a true Modoc!"

Several braves elbowed their way to her side, among them the young and handsome William Faithful, the man for whose life she was willing to pay with her own. They helped her down from the rock on which she stood, assuring her of protection, their actions and faces

speaking respect, even more eloquently than their
words.

Captain Jack ordered them to see her safely back
to headquarters. There were tears in Winema's eyes as
she said simply, "Thank you, Jack. You have acted
like a true man this day. I won't need your men to
guard me. I am not afraid to go back alone."

"No, they go with you, Winema," the Chief said.
"My men, some of them has evil hearts. You forget
words Jack spoke when he was mad. Jack, him your
friend."

Winema mounted her horse with his help. The rest
of the braves scattered while the little party moved off
down the trail. With four braves in front of her and
four behind, the "Woman-Chief-of-the-Brave Heart"
was escorted back to her anxious friends with a guard
of honor.

CHAPTER XI

TRAPPED

COMMISSION Chairman Meacham set out on the morning of April 10 to visit Colonel Mason's and Colonel Barnard's camp at the opposite southern extremity of the lake from Gillem's headquarters, leaving Reverend Thomas in charge of the commission during his absence.

While he was still at the other camp, the signal officer there picked up a message saying that a delegation of Modocs had arrived in Gillem's camp. Since this was a more or less frequent occurrence, Meacham gave it little thought. He talked over the situation in general with Mason and Barnard and found them skeptical of the possibility of further negotiations in view of the threat of treachery. It was late in the day before he returned to headquarters.

Meanwhile, Bogus and Boston Charley were making the most of his absence. They were well aware of the faith in God which Reverend Thomas professed. They knew, also, that he was too trusting to attribute anything but the best of motives to others and they were

General E. R. S. Canby

Rev. Eleazer Thomas

clever enough to take advantage of the opportunity to deal with him instead of Meacham.

"We change our hearts," they told Reverend Thomas. "God has put a new fire in us. We ashamed of bad hearts. We ready to do like you say. You come to council tent, leave guns here, we settle everything."

It never occurred to Thomas that they could be two-faced. To him it was evidence that his prayers had been answered. Moreover, he probably thought it would be a feather in his cap to be the one to arrange for the reconciliation. He accepted their words at face value and after a brief consultation with Canby, he convinced the general to agree to meet them unarmed.

When Meacham arrived in camp, he found Reverend Thomas jubilant. "God has done a wonderful work in the Modoc camp," he told Meacham.

The commission chairman was considerably upset by the development things had taken in his absence, and shocked the Reverend Mr. Thomas by saying in reply, "Bosh! God hasn't been near the Modoc camp all winter! If we go, we'll never come back alive!"

In order to be on hand to see that nothing occurred to prevent the consummation of their plans, Bogus stayed in Gillem's camp the night before the meeting was scheduled. Boston Charley arrived early the next morning.

The commissioners were still eating their breakfasts when they saw his head push aside the tent flap. Thomas rose to greet him and invited him to have something to eat. With a certain diabolical pleasure, Boston Charley accepted the invitation, and sat down at the very seat from which the man he had agreed to kill had just arisen. This man who had received so many presents of food and clothing from the "preacher man" ate the food they offered him from the same plate Thomas had used, drank his coffee from the same cup.

Boston Charley, the man with two tongues, knew which one to use and when. He talked of the peace that at last was to be made that day. He professed friendship for the commissioners with his lips, while his eyes and ears were alert to note the slightest indication of suspicion on the part of his hosts.

The meeting was set for noon. As the hour approached, the commissioners became more and more reluctant about going. The Modoc messengers became impatient at their slowness in getting ready. They pointed to the council tent with the words, "Cap'n Jack, him waiting now. Him and four others."

Up on the mountainside at the signal station, men were scanning the vicinity of the council tent with field glasses. Under orders from General Canby to keep the strictest watch on the tent and the trail leading to it, they had been at their post since the first rays of light had crept over the Lava Beds.

Little did they guess that two of the Modoc warriors had out-witted them by slipping out before daylight, secreting themselves behind rocks out of sight of the signal station. These men were Barncho and Slolux, each of whom had taken as many rifles as he could carry and now lay hidden from view.

As the sun, peeking through the gathering clouds, was almost half-way across the sky, the peace-makers gathered at General Gillem's tent. On the way, Meacham met Riddle, who anxiously pleaded with him to persuade the commissioners to stay in camp. "You mustn't go!" he protested. "If you go, you're sure to get killed!"

"Why don't you come over to General Gillem's tent and tell that to the rest of them," Meacham suggested.

When they arrived, they found General Gillem sick on his cot. The others were all there. Canby, who had been talking to Colonel Green outside, remarked from the tent door, "Go on, gentlemen. Don't wait for me. I'll be in presently."

Riddle repeated his warning. "Gentlemen, I've been talking to my wife. She's never told me a lie nor made things out to be worse than they are. She says if you go today, they'll kill every one of you. My advice is, don't do it! But in any case, be sure you're well armed! I'm telling you this because I don't want any blame for what happens. Tobey and I wash our hands of any responsibility if you're killed. We've warned you!"

Canby entered just as Riddle went out. The warning was repeated to him. The general was grave, but assured them, "I've had field glasses trained on the tent all morning. There are only four men at the council tent. The signal station detail are under strict orders to keep a close watch. If the Modocs should make an attack, I've arranged for the army to move in on them at once. With these precautions I think we'll be safe enough."

"Riddle and his wife are unduly excited," Thomas put in. "You can't depend on what they say under these circumstances. For my part, I'm determined to keep our word and leave every thing in the hands of God. I'm sure if we do our duty we can leave the rest to our Maker."

Meacham was extremely perturbed. "I differ with you, gentlemen. I think we ought to heed their warning. If we go, I'm for taking our pistols, at least. If we don't, we're almost sure to be attacked with no means of defending ourselves. It's all right to have the army back of us, but they'd be so far back we'd all be dead before they even got moving!"

"I agree with Meacham," Dyer said. "After the warnings we've had, we'd be fools to go unarmed."

"I've taken every precaution," Canby repeated. "I think the danger has been exaggerated and that we'll have no trouble with them at all."

"Yes, and the agreement was to leave our weapons behind. We must be faithful to our part of the agreement and trust in God," Reverend Thomas insisted.

Thomas and Canby prevailed and the group broke up to prepare for the trip to the council tent.

General Canby went to his own tent where he talked for some time in low tones to Scott, his orderly. When he reappeared, he was meticulously dressed in full uniform.

Reverend Thomas stopped at the camp store on the way to his own tent to pay for some goods he had bought for the Modocs the previous day. "I want to get all my obligations cleared up," he told the sutler. "I'm not too sure I'll return, but I mean to do my duty faithfully and trust in God to bring it out all right."

He returned shortly, dressed in a light gray tweed suit to join General Canby and await the others. They could overhear snatches of conversation between the officers and men who were standing around among the tents talking in low tones of the impending danger.

The soldiers differed considerably in their opinions, but on one thing they agreed. They were ready to fly to the rescue in case of treachery.

Meacham was in earnest conversation with Fairchild. "What do you think, John? Is it safe to go?"

"Wait a minute," he replied. "Let me have another

talk with Bogus. Maybe I can surprise him into saying something that may throw some light on it."

After a few minutes he returned, whittling on a stick. Slowly he shook his head. "I can't make out from Bogus what to think. I don't like the under-current of things. His talk seems all right, but I can't tell. It may be all on the square."

"Well, on the square or not, I've got to go if Canby and Thomas go," Meacham said, with certain resignation. He hurried to his tent. There he sat down on a roll of blankets and with a stub of a pencil, wrote hastily:

> "Lava Beds, April 11, 1873.
> My dear wife:
> You may be a widow tonight, but you shall not be a coward's wife. I go to save my honor. John Fairchild will forward my valise and valuables. The chances are all against us. I have done my best to prevent this meeting. I am nowise to blame.   Yours to the end,
> Alfred.
> P. S. I am giving Fairchild six hundred and fifty dollars in currency for you."

Then he sought out Fairchild once more, handed him the note and explained what he wanted him to do. "And John, I want you to promise me one thing on your sacred word of honor. Will you promise?"

Fairchild's gray eyes searched Meacham's face. "I promise you anything within my power."

"Then promise me that if my body is brought in mutilated you'll bury me here, so that my family will never be tortured by the sight."

"Oh, but you're going to come back all right . . . "

"But you'll promise what I ask in case I don't?"

"You can depend on me."

"Good. I tell you, John, there is but one alternative ... death or disgrace. I can die. But my name never has been and never will be dishonored!"

Fairchild drew a revolver from his hip. "Here, Meacham, take this. You can bang brimstone out of 'em with it if they start any monkey business."

"No, John ... no! I can't take it. I'd rather have it than all your cattle, but if I take that revolver everyone will swear that I provoked the fight by going armed contrary to the agreement. My reputation wouldn't be worth a cent if I took it. There's no use talking. I've got to go unarmed and I'm going."

Dyer approached the two men. He carried a small bundle in his hands. "Mr. Fairchild, I want to send this parcel to Mrs. Dyer. Would you please do that for me?"

Meacham turned to him. "Dyer, why don't you refuse to go? I certainly would if I were in your place. Being the chairman ͮ the peace commission, I have to go ... either go or be disgraced. But there's no necessity for your going."

"If you go, I'm going. It would be nothing short of cowardice not to go if all of the rest of you do."

A man passed close to Meacham and dropped something in his pocket. The commissioner's hand rested on it. For a moment his face revealed a mental conflict. The man whispered, "You may need it. It'll do the work, all right!" It was a small Derringer pistol and it remained in Meacham's pocket. Dyer noted the little maneuver. Quickly he went to his tent and slipped a Derringer into his own pocket.

Bogus and Boston were waiting, impatiently. Boston

Charley approached the little group with the words, "You come. Cap'n Jack, him get tired waiting."

Meacham turned away to get his horse. He found Winema clinging to the halter rope, weeping. "Tobey, give me my horse. I must go now," Meacham said, kindly.

"Meacham, you no go! You get kill! Me no give you your horse!" she cried, in her distress forgetting to speak as her husband had taught her. "Modocs mad now! They kill all you men!" Winding the rope around her body, she threw herself on the ground. In broken sobs she continued to exhort him.

"Meacham, you no go! You no go! Oh, you get kill! I know you get kill!"

Meacham's lips quivered, although he tried hard to maintain his self-control. His face paled. He stood there watching Winema, listening to Winema, struggling with his pride.

His pride gave way. He would make one more effort to avert the doom that threatened them. He called to Thomas and Canby just as they were ready to start off on foot. They stopped and waited for him.

He placed a hand on each man's shoulder. "Gentlemen, my deliberate opinion is that if we go to the council tent today we'll be carried back on stretchers, hacked to pieces. I tell you, I think Tobey is right. We can't afford to ignore her warning."

"Meacham, you're unduly cautious," Canby chided him. "There are only five Indians at the council tent, and they wouldn't dare attack us!"

"General, the Modocs dare anything! I know them better than you do, and I know they're desperate. Braver men and worse men never lived than we are to meet at that council tent!"

"I've left orders for the army to advance at the least indication of danger," Canby replied. "We've agreed to meet them, and we must."

"We can't go back on our compact," Thomas interposed. "We are in the hands of God, and if he requires our lives we should be glad to make the sacrifice."

"Well, if you insist on going, at least let's not go utterly defenseless!"

"Brother Meacham, that is the agreement, and we must abide by it."

"But the Modocs will be armed to the teeth! You can be sure of that. They'll never keep their part of the agreement. Let Fairchild go with us. John and I with a revolver each might be able to prevent a terrible slaughter. I won't object to going under those circumstances. I know Fairchild. He's a dead shot. He and I could out-shoot those Indians in the open any time."

"Brother Meacham, you and Fairchild are fighting men. We are going to make peace, not war. Let us go as we agreed and trust in God!"

"That may be all right, but God doesn't drop revolvers into your hands just when you need them!"

"My dear brother, you are getting blasphemous. Put your trust in your Maker. You should pray more and think less about fighting."

"Thomas, I'm just as much of a peace man as you are. I'm as good a friend as these Indians ever had. I know where to put my trust in dealing with them. I've known these Modocs for years. And you can bet they won't leave their guns behind. I tell you, we've got to be ready for trouble when it comes."

"That's what we agreed to, and we mustn't jeopardize our lives by breaking our word. If they have evil intentions, it will give them just the excuse they're looking for."

Meacham realized it was hopeless to try to influence them on that score. He tried another tack. "Well, since we must go unarmed, I'm for granting them any demand they make rather than give them an excuse to murder us! That is, if they're armed . . . and they will be!"

General Canby's tall, straight figure stiffened. "Mr. Meacham, I've had more or less connection with the Indian service for thirty years. I've never made a promise I couldn't carry out. I'm not willing to promise anything we can't perform."

"Nor I," Thomas broke in. "That's just why the Indians have so little confidence in white men!"

"But listen, gentlemen!" Meacham pleaded. "I only propose to do so in case they've broken their part of the compact. I don't believe in false promises any more than you do, except in such an event. It may mean life or death! I tell you, I'd promise an Indian anything before I'd give him an excuse to take your lives and mine. I say it isn't dishonest, and my conscience would never condemn me for saving five lives by such strategy!"

Both Canby and Thomas stood their ground. Meacham was forced to realize that his efforts to prevent the meeting had failed. He turned slowly away and took a few hesitating steps toward his horse. The other two commissioners started off, side by side.

Still Meacham could not give up. Before they had gone many steps, he turned. "Gentlemen, once more I implore you not to go. I for one, have too much to live for. Too many are dependent on me. I have no desire to die. If I go it will be only to save my name from dishonor."

"That squaw's got you scared, Meacham. I don't see why you should be so careful of your scalp! With your bald spot, you haven't as much to lose as I have!" Canby chaffed.

"Yes, I'll admit she has me scared. That's true! I am afraid. I have reason to be, and if you weren't so stubborn you'd know that you have too!"

This time, Meacham went back to his anxious friends, waiting at the tent. He had lost the usual quickness of movement characteristic of him. His footsteps lagged. But he was firm. His tightly set lips declared that his mind was made up.

Winema was still sobbing, still clinging to the halter. She refused to let go until the sternness of Meacham's command forced her to do so. She dropped the rope and grasped his coat, repeating her plea. "You no go, Meacham. Say you no go. You get kill, sure!"

"Let go, Tobey. Get on your horse. There's no way out. We've got to make the best of it!"

Riddle was pale, but cool and collected. "I'm goin' afoot," he said quietly. "I don't want a horse to get in my way."

The Indian woman embraced her boy again and again, before she could finally bring herself to mount her horse. At last they were off.

"Goodbye, boys! Goodbye, Fairchild! Be sure to come for us if we need you!"

"We'll have an eye out for you," Fairchild called. "Goodbye and good luck!"

CHAPTER XII

"OT-WE-KAU-TUX-E!"

AT the peace tent the waiting Modocs became restless. Noon, the hour set for the meeting, had come and gone with no sun to mark its passing. Glowering clouds pressed a heavy silence down over the rocks . . . a silence that was portentous, charged with foreboding until it seemed itself an evil presence.

Captain Jack sat on a rock near the small sagebrush fire, staring at his moccasin clad feet with a detached expression. Ellen's Man moved from the path of the low-lying, pungent smoke that veered from the fire and sat down near the Chief, his coffee-colored, full-moon face alight with anticipation like a young boy playing a game.

Captain Jack spoke, more to himself than to Ellen's Man. His voice was low, husky. "Me no feel right to kill those mans," he muttered.

Ellen's Man glanced scornfully at his Chief. "You show white feather!" he chided. "You have heart like rabbit. You 'fraid, me kill Canby!"

"No! Jack's heart is brave. Me kill soldier ty-ee. But it do Modocs no good!"

Not far away sat Schonchin John, drawing queer pictures in the dirt with a stick while a hard, cunning look played about his mouth and eyes, bespeaking the lust to kill. Hooker Jim was too excited to sit still, pacing back and forth with the cat-like movements of a tiger in a cage, and nervously fingering a string of deer teeth which dangled from his neck. Shacknasty Jim crouched on his heels staring in the direction of Gillem's camp, his whole attitude resembling a wild beast about ready to spring upon his prey.

Forty or fifty paces away from the council tent in the direction of the Modoc camp, Barncho and Slolux were concealed, numbed with cold, behind a low ledge of rocks, a pile of rifles lying beside them. Their bodies ached from their long wait since early morning on the sharp rocks, and they were even more impatient for action than their fellows.

Scarface Charley was not far away, hidden from view by a low clump of sagebrush. He was hoping that the commissioners wouldn't come at all, for he was there for one purpose and one purpose only . . . to back up his words in regard to Winema and Frank Riddle.

Shacknasty Jim suddenly sprang to his feet as he caught sight of Bogus Charley coming down the trail at a half-trot.

"They come!" Bogus announced. "They leave guns behind. We kill them peace-mans easy!"

Boston Charley was close on his heels with General Canby and Reverend Thomas not far behind. The Indians greeted the two men cordially . . . too cordially. Canby returned their greeting, and from a box carried under his arm, passed cigars which were accepted with profuse expressions of gratitude.

The Modocs lit them from a point of flame at the end of a sagebrush twig, salvaged from the fire, and were smoking with the greatest show of friendliness when Meacham's party approached. Meacham reined his horse to the right of the council tent while Dyer and Winema drew up to the left. Frank Riddle, on foot, passed in front of the shelter, peering in as he did so. It was empty and a fleeting expression of relief crossed his face.

Even before the party had a chance to dismount, the Indians came extending their hands in demonstration of friendship. But Meacham saw more than their extended hands and friendly manner. He noted that the council fire had been moved from its former position and was placed so that the tent stood between it and the signal station; that there were no squaws present, as there had always been before; and that every Indian showed evidence of a revolver secreted beneath his clothing. Yet he gave no hint that he mistrusted the Modocs. He returned their greetings warmly and took off his overcoat as if to make himself more comfortable . . . 'though in reality, he did so because the little Derringer pistol was in the pocket of his suit coat.

Dyer, the first to alight from his horse, was pale, but otherwise showed no evidence of the see-saw struggle between his pride and his fear. Winema slid quietly from her pony and tied it to a small sagebrush near the tent. Meacham dismounted, but changed his mind about securing the rope when he surprised a gloating look in Shacknasty Jim's eyes as they rested on his well-groomed horse. He decided that at least the splendid animal of which he had learned to think a great deal should have a chance to escape so he left the halter loose upon the ground.

As the group gathered around the council fire, there was an undercurrent of tension as they maneuvered for positions, the Modocs trying to separate themselves from the commissioners so that their targets would be unobstructed, while Dyer, Riddle and Meacham were determined to prevent it. Canby stood erect and apparently indifferent to the pantomime being played around him. Reverend Thomas, too, seemed oblivious to it. Either he did not realize its significance or his faith in God was so sustaining that he considered such actions mere foolishness.

Finding that the Modocs thwarted every attempt to mix with them, and positive now that his worst fears were justified, Meacham turned with a careless air and took a few steps in the direction of the soldiers' camp, vaguely hoping that he might be able to signal those at the lookout station. But that hope, too, was frustrated. Always beside him was a pair of beady eyes . . . Hooker Jim's eyes . . . watching every movement, while glibly calling attention to the storm clouds massed over the nearby hills.

No outward sign marred the unusually good-humored front the Modocs assumed, yet Meacham soon sensed the restlessness of Captain Jack and his braves. And indeed, he himself was anxious to have it over with for anything would be better than this harrowing suspense. He strolled over to the fire and sat down on a rock which was taken as a signal that the council was ready to begin. As they seated themselves, the Modocs, as before, were careful to separate themselves from their intended victims. Canby selected a rock at Meacham's right while Thomas bent a small sagebrush, placed his overcoat on it, and sat down a little to the left and slightly back of Meacham.

"Tobey," Meacham began, "Tell your people that we came here to-day to hear what they have to propose. They sent for us, and we are ready to conclude the terms of peace as their messengers requested."

Winema, seated on the ground in front of Thomas, faithfully translated Meacham's words into "Mo-a-doc-us ham-konk" (the Modoc language) while her husband interpreted the Modoc replies into "Boston talk".

To Meacham's words Captain Jack replied pointedly, "We want no more war. We are tired. Our women and children are afraid of the soldiers. We want them taken away and *then* we can make peace."

"General Canby is in charge of the soldiers," Meacham told him. "He is your friend. He came here because the Great White Father sent him to look out for everybody and see that everything goes all right."

"We do not want the soldiers here. They make our hearts afraid. Send them away and we can make everything all right."

"General Canby cannot take the soldiers away without a letter from the President. You needn't be afraid. We are all your friends. We can find a better place for you than this where you can live in peace. If you are willing to come out of the rocks and go with us, we will take you for a little while to Angel island in San Francisco bay and leave the women and children in camp over on Hot Creek. Then we shall need the soldiers to make other folks stay away from them while we hunt up a new home for you."

As this was being interpreted, Meacham's attention was caught by a sideplay that was going on behind Captain Jack. Hooker Jim had been pacing back and forth, first intently scanning the rocks in the direction of the soldiers' camp, then sauntering back to the edge of the group, always keeping in front of the white men.

This time Meacham saw him go to his horse, stoop down and secure the halter to a sagebrush, pushing the knot close to the ground. Rising slowly, Hooker Jim called the animal by name and told him he was a "fine horse". With his eyes fixed on Meacham, Hooker Jim picked up the overcoat which had been thrown across the saddle. Assuming an air of bravado, he slipped his left arm in the sleeve. Then without shifting his eyes from Meacham's face or changing his position, he quickly thrust his right arm in the other sleeve and shrugged the coat squarely onto his shoulders.

Buttoning it up from top to bottom, he took a step toward the fire. He interrupted Winema, pounding himself on the chest with his fist, showing his white teeth in a crooked grin. "Me old man Meacham, now! Bogus, you no think me look like old man Meacham?"

The commissioner realized there was a reason for Hooker securing the horse and that it wasn't for his, Meacham's, benefit! He also knew that Hooker Jim was trying to start something . . . something that would precipitate a quarrel. He tried to appear indifferent and treat it all as a joke.

"Hooker Jim, you'd better take my hat, too!" he offered, taking it from his head and holding it out toward him.

A sly, knowing glance accompanied the redskin's reply. "No. Sno-ker gam-bla sit-ka caitch-con-a bos-ti-na chock-i-la! (I will by and by. Don't hurry, old man!)"

Every white man's face blanched a shade whiter at this, yet no word of fear was spoken. Dyer, his features

set as if carved in marble, rose and walked slowly to
his horse, pretending to adjust the cinch. He was careful to keep the horse between himself and the Modocs,
his face toward the council group. Riddle, pale and
nervous, made an excuse to change the fastenings on
his wife's pony which stood behind Reverend Thomas.
Both Dyer and Riddle intended to be covered when
they started their dash for life.

Winema stretched herself full length on the ground
with a child-like yawn, her chin resting on her hands.
She evidently had no desire to be in the way of any
bullets that might fly if she could help it.

For seconds, these arbiters who knew their lives were
at stake waited in silence, not knowing how their fate
would come. They tensed to meet it . . . but nothing
happened. The only movement was that of the great
black clouds being driven closer before a rising wind
and casting a sombre twilight over the Lava Beds,
although it was still mid-afternoon.

Desperately hoping that General Canby understood
the great peril of the moment and would promise anything to avert tragedy, Meacham nodded to him to
speak. Canby, who had remained stoically in his place,
rose to his feet. Every eye was fixed on him for the
Modocs recognized him as the white man's ty-ee. He
towered above the others, poised, apparently fearless.
Only his slightly quivering lower lip indicated the intensity of his emotions. Slowly he spoke.

"Tobey, tell these people that the President of the
United States sent the soldiers here to protect them as
well as the white men. They are all friends of the
Indians. They cannot be taken away without the consent
of the President.

"Tell them that when I was a young man, I vas

sent to move a band of Indians from their old home to a new one. They did not like me at first, but when they became better acquainted they liked me so well they made me a chief. They gave me a name that meant 'Friend-of-the-Indian'.

"I also moved another tribe to a new home. They, too, made me a chief and gave me a name that meant 'The-Tall-Man'. Many years afterwards I visited these people. They came a long distance to meet me and were very glad to see me. Tell them I have no doubt that sometime the Modocs will like me as those Indians did and recognize me as their friend."

The general bowed his head gravely and sat down. Meacham turned to Reverend Thomas and invited him to speak. The "Sunday Doctor" dropped forward on one knee, resting his right hand on Meacham's shoulder and said, "Tobey, tell these people for me that I believe the Great Spirit put it into the heart of the President to send us here to make peace. We are all children of one Father. Our hearts are all open to Him. He sees all we do. He knows all our hearts. We are brothers.

"I have known these men a long time. General Canby eight years, Meacham fourteen years, Mr. Dyer four years. I know their hearts are good. We do not want any more bloodshed. We want to be your friends. God sees all we do. He will hold us responsible for what we do."

An uneasy silence followed after Thomas had resumed his seat and Winema had interpreted his words. Captain Jack had lost his usual composure, appearing ill at ease and nervous. His men were watching him closely as if they mistrusted him. Indeed, Meacham had almost made up his mind that the Chief was wavering.

For several seconds the two men, Meacham and Captain Jack, stared into each other's eyes, each meeting a gaze as intense as his own.

Suddenly Jack jerked himself erect as if trying to shake off a bad dream. He turned his back on the white men, took several steps and stopped. As he did so, Schonchin John leapt into the place occupied by the Chief a moment before. Eyes gleaming, voice rasping with hatred, he demanded, "Give Modocs Hot Creek for home! Give us Hot Creek and take away soldier mans!"

Meacham spoke calmly, trying to take the heat from Schonchin's words with the coolness of his own. "We would like to do that, but it belongs to Fairchild and Press Dorris. We can see them about it and if they agree you may have it."

"If! You say always 'if'!" Schonchin shouted, his bronzed face flushed with anger. "Take away your Bosteena soldiers and give us Hot Creek or quit talking! We tired talking. We talk no more!"

Schonchin John flung out this ultimatum with a snarl. Captain Jack, standing close behind him, lifted his hand and gave a signal that brought a warwhoop from every redskin. The commissioners were on their feet as if they'd been released by springs.

"What does this mean, Jack?" Meacham cried.

In answer the Modoc Chief drew a sixshooter from under his left arm and flourished it in the air. "Ot-we-kau-tux-e! (All ready!)" he shouted.

At the words, Barncho and Slolux came running with as many rifles as they could carry under each arm. The other Modocs drew revolvers and closed in on the white men. Captain Jack pointed his gun at General Canby's head and pulled the trigger. The cap exploded with a dull click, but failed to touch off the powder. Thei c was a moment's chance for the general to make a run for it, but, true to the traditions of the army, he stood unflinching.

Captain Jack set the hammer on another bullet and fired. The shot sped true to its mark, striking Canby in the head. He staggered, ran several steps, collapsed on the sharp rocks, shattering his lower jaw.

Other shots rang out. The bullets from Boston Charley's revolver pierced Thomas above the heart. He dropped, checking his fall with his right arm. With his other hand raised in supplication, he implored Boston Charley not to shoot again.

At Captain Jack's signal, Schonchin John closed with Meacham. Like a flash, he drew his revolver with one hand and unsheathed a knife with the other, since he was so close to his victim he dare not trust to the gun alone. In his excitement he fumbled. It was Meacham's chance. He drew his Derringer, aimed it at Schonchin's heart and pressed the trigger. The hammer stuck, the gun missed fire.

Schonchin struck at his opponent with his knife, but missed as Meacham ducked and stepped back. As he did so, Schonchin fired and the bullet ripped through the commissioner's coat collar, grazing his shoulder. Meacham turned and ran with Schonchin in pursuit, emptying his gun at him.

Meanwhile, Dyer was making a breathless dash toward the soldier's camp with Hooker Jim and Black Jim after him. Their whistling bullets lent wings to Dyer's feet. The pursued man turned, aimed his Derringer at Hooker and fired. Hooker dropped to the ground to avoid the shot. Although the bullet missed, Dyer lengthened his lead as Black Jim helped Hooker scramble to his feet again. Having emptied their guns to no avail, the redskins gave up the chase and returned to help their fellow murderers at the council tent.

Riddle made straight for the lake with Shacknasty Jim in pursuit, firing shots in rapid succession, but obviously wide of their mark, for from the corner of his eyes he could see Scarface Charley watching with rifle leveled. He knew that if he struck Riddle, he in turn would fall by a shot from Scarface. After a half-hearted chase, he fell back, but Riddle didn't slacken his pace for an instant.

When Canby fell, Ellen's Man pounced on him like a wolf on his prey. The general was still writhing in the death struggle when Captain Jack pinned his shoulders to the ground, while Ellen's Man slashed his throat with a knife. Not waiting even until his heart had ceased to beat, they stripped off his uniform. Captain Jack placed Canby's hat on his own head, strapped the general's sword around his waist. As Barncho came up, Ellen's Man snatched a rifle from him, placed the muzzle against the prostrate man's head and pulled the trigger. They left him sprawled on his face while they gathered up his uniform and trappings.

Bogus and Boston Charley allowed Thomas to struggle to his feet and start to run. Bogus tripped him. He fell. They taunted him with the words, "Why your God no turn bullets? You no got strong medicine!" Pleading with them to spare his life, and with God to soften their hearts, Thomas rose and stumbled on a few steps. His tormentors sent their benefactor sprawling with a blow. They laughed in his face. "Next time you believe squaw! Your God no good. Him weak like 'Sunday Doctor'!"

Another attempt to rise was followed by another

brutal blow. Bogus grabbed a rifle from Slolux, placed the muzzle against the man's head, sent a bullet crashing through it.

"Come, Lord . . . " Thomas gasped, but the prayer was smothered by his own blood.

Schonchin emptied one pistol at Meacham then drew another from his belt. Winema, who had flattened herself to the ground at the first shot, jumped up and ran after Schonchin, grabbed his arm just as he was again about to fire. He tried to fling her off, but she clung desperately.

"No kill Meacham! No kill him!" she cried. "Him your friend. Him friend of Indians!"

Winema's interference gave Meacham a moment to widen the distance between himself and his pursuer. Slolux joined Schonchin and struck Winema on the head with the butt of a rifle. It dazed her a moment but she didn't fall.

Shacknasty Jim grasped a rifle Slolux handed him, crouched and took deliberate aim at Meacham. "Me get him!" he grunted.

Glancing over his shoulder, Meacham saw Shacknasty. Without stopping, he pounded his chest. "Shoot me there, you red devil!" he cried.

Winema struck down the gun just as Shacknasty pulled the trigger. Schonchin gripped her arms while she squirmed and struggled to free herself. Again Shacknasty took aim and this time his bullet went straight, catching Meacham near the shoulder blade just as he leapt over a low ledge of rocks and fell.

"Me hit him high up! Him done for!" Shacknasty gloated.

Already wounded in several places and fast weakening from loss of blood, Meacham decided to fire his

only shot. Edging the pistol up over the edge of the
rocks, he raised his head ever so slightly. He saw
Schonchin crouching, saw the revolver in his hand.

The two fired simultaneously. Schonchin crumpled,
wounded on the rocks. Meacham felt a blinding sting
and lightning flashed in his brain as Schonchin's bullet
caught him under the eyebrow. The stunned man staggered drunkenly. His pistol dropped from his hand.
Dazed, he exposed himself as a perfect target for
Shacknasty's rifle. One ball tore away the lobe of his
ear. Another glanced from the right side of his head,
leaving an ugly groove where it passed. He sank to the
ground, his limbs quivering.

Shacknasty was the first to reach Meacham, who was
unconscious. Off came the boots, coat, trousers. Shacknasty had no use for the man's vest so he tore it down
the side and threw it away. Carefully he removed the
shirt, for it was a new one and just Shacknasty's size.
While he was unbuttoning it, Slolux placed the
barrel of a rifle close to the wounded man's temple, in-
tending to dispatch him, as they had the others.

Shacknasty pushed it away. In the Modoc tongue he
growled, "You needn't shoot. Him dead. Him no get
up after Shacknasty shoot him!"

Above the wild shouting of his braves as they performed these fiendish tasks, Captain Jack's voice rang
out, calling them back to the council tent. Shacknasty
and Slolux, having secured all the loot they could from
Meacham, left Winema on her knees at the bleeding
man's side.

"Him your dead brother, you white-hearted squaw!"
they taunted. "How you like him now?"

As the assassins gathered around their Chief with the
red, blood-stained clothing in their hands, the blackness of

unnatural night seemed to close in on the Lava Beds. In this terrifying gloom, General Canby stiffened on the rocks. Reverend Thomas, half nude, was still convulsing in the grip of death. Meacham lay still and oblivious to Winema's tears falling on his upturned face.

Captain Jack ordered his crew of cut-throats back to the stronghold. Hastily they helped the wounded Schonchin John onto Meacham's horse. Canby's uniform, Thomas' suit and Meacham's clothes and overcoat were lashed on Dyer's horse.

The others had started back to the stronghold when Barncho, who had lingered behind, grasped the reins of Winema's horse. He cursed because it bore a lady's side saddle. He was awkwardly trying to mount when Winema saw him.

She rushed from Meacham's side, caught Barncho by the coat tails and nearly threw him to the ground. "You no take my horse!" she cried.

Barncho was infuriated. He picked up his gun that had fallen at his feet and struck Winema with it between the shoulders, knocking her to the ground. "You white man's sister!" he snarled. "Me leave you with dead brothers. You bother me no more!"

As he turned back to the horse, Winema staggered to her feet. She picked up a large rock and threw it at Barncho with all her might. He fell to his knees. "You coward!" she screamed. "You fight with woman! You never take my horse. You kill me first!"

Barncho brought his gun to his shoulder. "All right! I kill you!" he blazed.

A heavy hand fell on his shoulder and whirled him around. He stared into the muzzle of a revolver in the hands of Captain Jack, whose words lashed out like a whip.

"If we no need you so bad in war with paleface, I blow your head off and leave you here for buzzards!" he threatened, using the forceful dialect of the Modocs. "What you mean to strike that woman? Give back horse to Winema and get out of my sight quick!"

Barncho dropped the halter rope as if it were a deadly snake and slunk away without saying a word.

Boston Charley took advantage of this interruption for purposes of his own. "Me go get old man Meacham's scalp to put on shot-pouch," he told Shacknasty Jim.

"Him no got scalp!" Shacknasty chuckled. "Him have scalp, me have it long before now!"

Nevertheless, Boston Charley ran to where the bleeding man was lying. He took from his pocket a small, dull-bladed knife, a memento taken from a soldier killed in the battle in the fog. Placing his foot on the prostrate man's head, he made a gash from his left ear to the center of his forehead.

"Hmph!" he grunted. "Old man Meacham, him got plenty tough hide!"

Winema, no longer preoccupied with saving her horse, caught sight of Boston Charley. She ran back to Meacham and tried to intercede on his behalf. Impelled by the memory of what Meacham had done for her, she could not restrain herself. She tried to interfere but Boston Charley thrust her aside and renewed his efforts to secure a new ornament for his belt.

He cursed Meacham's baldness, but swore he would take one ear to make up for the lack of hair. Holding the head with his left hand, he cut squarely down to the skull with a long, half-circular gash intended to remove sidelock, ear and all.

Unable to accomplish her purpose by physical means,

Winema resorted to strategy. Jumping up, she clapped her hands and shouted, "'Bosteena soldiers! Kot-pum-bla! (The soldiers are coming!)"

Startled, Boston Charley dropped his knife and fled. Winema's warning words reached the ears of the others. Without stopping to look back, every man made a wild dash across the rocks toward their camp, fully expecting the soldiers to be upon them any moment.

Winema knelt down and wiped the blood from the face of the man whose scalp she had saved. She pressed her hand over his heart. "It stop! It stop!" she moaned. Gently she straightened the man's limbs, placed his hands across his breast and stood for a few moments, choking back her sobs, before mounting her horse and riding with all speed toward the soldier's camp.

CHAPTER XIII

HANGED IN EFFIGY

THE scene of terror at the council tent was not the only one being enacted on that eleventh day of April, 1873. On the opposite side of the Modoc stronghold, Curly Head Doctor and Curly Jack were carrying out their part of the Modocs' bloody plan.

Displaying a flag of truce, they approached Colonel Mason's camp to trick the "Little Ty-ee" into meeting them among the rocks. But he was not to be fooled. His long experience with Indian fighting plus the events of the last few days had made him wary, and he refused to meet the two braves.

Major Boyle was on hand, however, and in spite of Meacham's warnings in regard to threatened treachery, he volunteered to go out to meet them under the flag of truce. He persuaded Lieutenant Sherwood to go with him and they secured Mason's consent, confident that they could handle any situation which might arise. Instructing the guards to keep a close watch, they advanced cautiously and soon left the picket line behind.

When within hailing distance, Boyle called out, "What do you want?"

"Want talk with Little Ty-ee," Curly Head Doctor shouted back.

"The colonel sent us in his place," Boyle answered. "What can we do for you?"

Before the Indians could reply, the major's sharp eyes caught sight of a gun concealed behind the flag of truce. The only answer they received was the sharp crack of an Indian's musket. Boyle yelled at Sherwood, "Run! Run for your life!"

Both men turned and fled with bullets whistling about their ears. They had gone only a few yards when Sherwood gave a sharp cry of agony, staggered, fell, his thigh shattered by a ball from Curly Jack's gun.

At the sound of the shots the guards rushed to the rescue of the wounded man, routed the two redskins, who ducked and dodged from rock to rock, in their retreat to the stronghold.

From the signal station at Mason's camp flashed the message, "Boyle and Sherwood attacked under flag of truce!" The signal officer stationed on the bluff dictated the message to his orderly. The hastily written words were sent post-haste to General Gillem in the camp a hundred yards below.

The general, still lying ill on his cot, read the dispatch and ordered the messenger to forward it with all possible speed to the peace commissioners at the council tent. He had not finished giving his instructions when another messenger came rushing down the hill, shouting, "The commissioners! The Modocs are firing on the commissioners!"

Instantly the officers mustered their troops. "Fall in! Fall in!" rang through the camp. The bugle repeated the call. Soldiers rushed to their positions, five hundred of them, ready for orders to march on the Modocs.

General Gillem, trying to shake off the grip of illness, hesitated. He seemed bewildered. Another man rushed from the signal station. "I saw Canby fall!" he cried.

Still no command from Gillem. The men were frantic. Officers swore and threatened to move without orders. At last the general shook off his lethargy. "Forward, march!" he shouted. "Spread out from the left in skirmish line!"

"Double-quick, forward march!" The command barked down the lines while the bugle sounded. "Forward!"

The soldiers surged across the rocks, followed by surgeons and orderlies bearing stretchers. In a few minutes they saw Dyer running toward them, shouting breathlessly, "They killed 'em all! All of 'em but me!"

Onward the troopers pushed. Suddenly Riddle appeared from his hiding place behind some rocks. "They are all dead!" he rasped out.

In a few moments they came upon Winema, the tears streaming down her face. "Canby, Thomas, Meacham, all kill!" she sobbed.

Nearly thirty minutes had elapsed after the first shot was fired before the soldiers closed in on the council tent. As they approached, Meacham, of whose life Winema had despaired, was struggling weakly to sit up. At the sight of the mutilated figure, the men near the center of the line leveled their guns.

"A damn Modoc!" shouted one of the troopers.

"No! Don't shoot!" bellowed an officer. "It's a white man!"

The soldiers surged past, as Meacham fell back on the cold rocks, exhausted.

"Here! Bring a stretcher!" ordered Dr. Cabaniss, in charge of the medical corps. "It's Meacham. He's still alive! If we work fast we may be able to save him. Easy, boys!"

The wounded man was groaning and mumbling incoherently as the orderlies lifted his body onto a stretcher. Hastily the surgeon probed his many wounds.

"Am I . . . going . . . to die?" Meacham faltered.

"You may pull through. Depends on whether you're wounded internally," Cabaniss snapped. "Now boys, for the hospital. Quick. Lose no time. We may save him!"

"I hit . . . Schonchin. He fell . . . I saw him . . ." The words came feebly as Meacham gasped for breath.

"Never mind about Schonchin," Cabaniss snorted. "We'll look out for him. Now hustle, boys, off with him!"

The stretcher was lifted by four strong pairs of arms. Four other men carried the guns and walked beside to relieve the carriers. One of them covered Meacham with his coat as they hurried along.

The soldiers found no signs of a Modoc at or near the peace tent. They scoured the rocks for hundreds of yards around, but in vain. All that greeted them was death . . . death, in the still forms of General Canby and Reverend Thomas.

A sharp cry rose above the shouts of the soldiers as young Scott, Canby's orderly, caught sight of the general. Scott had been with Canby in the Civil war, he had worshipped him, loved him, as he would his own father. At the sight of his prostrate form, he was frantic with grief and started raving like a mad man.

Orderlies with stretchers came up. Two of them picked up the body of the beloved commander and placed it on the canvas litter. Bill Dad pulled out a jackknife and slashed a large piece of canvas from the council tent with which to cover the still form . . . the peace tent, the general's winding sheet!

A piece of the canvas was also thrown over the stretcher on which lay the now-stiffened body of Reverend Thomas, then the grief-laden procession moved back toward camp.

Meanwhile, the quartermaster at the camp was moving quickly from place to place, seeing that the hospital was ready to receive patients, ordering food prepared for the fighting forces, packing mules with supplies, stretchers, water casks. In record time everything was ready and awaiting the commanding general's orders to follow up the pursuit of the Modocs.

No orders came. Instead, the glistening bayonets among the rocks drew nearer. The army of five hundred men was returning to camp!

"What in the devil does this mean?" fumed the quartermaster.

"Why in hell don't they go ahead and slaughter those damned redskins!" railed the officers, left in camp on guard.

"We shall not be ready to advance to the attack until the Warm Spring Indians arrive," announced General Gillem . . . the same General Gillem who a few days before had boasted that he could "take the Modocs out of their stronghold with the loss of half a dozen men."

Along with the darkness that night a heavy sense of grief and desperation settled over the isolated camps on the edge of the Lava Beds. From the tent nearest General Canby's late headquarters, the anguished sobs of

Orderly Scott mingled with repeated vows of vengeance. Face drawn, eyes wild, the bewildered young man at last rose from the side of his dead commander and was hurried away by friends lest he be completely overcome by his paroxysms of grief.

In the hospital tent Meacham was tenaciously clinging to life in spite of the greatest odds. He had been unconscious when Dr. Cabaniss and Dr. Semig started dressing his wounds by the light of a lamp held by a steward. The ragged, painful gash on the side of his face was carefully cleaned, sewed up and bandaged. Silver threads closed the gaping, crooked cut on the left side of his head that had nearly removed his scalp. With neat, careful stitches, his ear was patched up.

While the surgeon was probing the hole in his right arm, left by Schonchin John's bullet, Meacham began to regain consciousness. The ball had struck near the wrist, passed between the bones of his forearm and emerged midway between hand and elbow. By the time that wound was dressed and the doctors had the man's left arm stretched out on a board, Meacham was sufficiently aware of things to over-hear them agree that the forefinger must be amputated.

"Make out the line of the cut, doctor," he said, thickly.

"There, about this way," the doctor replied, tracing a line that ran nearly to the wrist.

"You can't do that without giving me chloroform. I couldn't stand it!"

The surgeon felt his pulse. "You're too weak to take chloroform. You've lost too much blood."

"Then let it stay until I'm stronger," Meacham begged.

The doctors consulted and decided that it should be

allowed to remain as it was. Aside, but not so low as to prevent Meacham from hearing, one of them remarked, "Well, after all, it won't disfigure a corpse very much!"

The truth was that Meacham himself felt that he hadn't long to live. A whisper from him brought one of the stewards to his cot. "Please ask General Gillem to send to Linkville for my brother-in-law, Captain Ferree," came from his bloodless lips.

"He should be here any time now," the steward replied. "The general sent a courier for him some time ago."

The wounded man smiled his appreciation of Gillem's thoughtfulness and again lapsed into unconsciousness. When he revived, Captain Ferree was standing over him. "He'll be blind if he recovers, won't he doctor?" the man was saying.

"We can't tell," the surgeon replied grimly. "But it's a sure bet he won't be very handsome!"

Through the long night, the pounding of hammers and the rasping of saws allowed no one to forget the awful happenings of the day. Everyone knew what those sounds meant. They came from the carpenters, fashioning gun cases into coffins. By morning two of them were ready, another begun. The latter was for Meacham, for it seemed impossible that he could survive the effect of his many wounds.

The bodies of General Canby and Reverend Thomas were gently placed in the pine boxes. The army, under command of Colonel Green, answered the bugle call for assembly, and lined up to receive the remains with the customary salute and muffled military music. There was scarcely a man who did not have to fight back the tears from his eyes and the lump in his throat, as eight commissioned officers and six sergeants, detailed as pall-bearers for General Canby and Reverend Thomas respectively, lifted up their coffins and marched toward the foot of the trail leading up the bluff, escorted by two artillery batteries as an escort of honor.

The funeral procession moved slowly up the steep path, at the top of which the pall-bearers' burdens were consigned to the wagons that were ready to start them on their way to Yreka. Accompanied by twenty cavalry-men and the faithful Scott, who refused to leave his dead commander, the improvised hearses moved off across the rugged plateau, leaving behind them the grief-stricken army.

Word reached Yreka on Sunday in advance of the slow-moving wagons that the remains of Canby and Thomas were only a few miles away. As if by spontaneous impulse, the townspeople marched out to meet them. When the cavalry escort came into view, the citizens formed in two lines on opposite sides of the road and stood with bared heads while the wagons and soldiers passed between them, then they closed in behind and the cortege moved slowly into Yreka, up Miner street to Masonic hall where arrangements had been made for the reception of the bodies.

All flags were exhibited at half mast while practically the whole population walked solemnly past the zinc-lined coffins to which the bodies had been transferred after embalming. A dirge-like atmosphere hung over the town until Monday afternoon when Canby's remains were started by the California and Oregon stage to Portland and Thomas' by private conveyance to San Francisco.

Only after they had gone did all the pent-up indignation of the townspeople, at this latest outrage, burst into full force. On every street corner, in every home, and every place where men gathered, there was but one thought voiced: That the whole treacherous Modoc tribe should meet a "swift and terrible retribution at the hands of the avenging soldiery."

Even stronger and louder than the prayers for revenge, however, were the curses heaped on the head of C. Delano, secretary of the interior and alleged author of the policy which substituted the "pow-wow" method for muskets and cannon. Feeling against him ran so high that the Yrekans held a mass meeting during which an effigy of Delano was hung from a rope stretched across the main street and fastened to the democratic and the republican flagpoles on opposite sides. On the front of the effigy hung a placard on which was printed, "C. Delano, Secretary of the Interior"; on the back another read, "The Quaker Indian Policy"; and a long card attached to the feet was inscribed, "Make Peace if it Takes All Summer. Signed: C. Delano."

All over the country a similar reaction took place as news of the massacre hummed along telegraph wires, poured from a thousand presses and was shouted by newsboys from every street corner. Those who had opposed the idea of trying to bring the Modocs to terms made the most of the opportunity to say, "I told you so." Even people who had formerly favored the "pow-wow policy" now raised a cry for "war . . . war to the last man!"

In sharp contrast to the magnitude of the problem they presented to the public mind, the Modocs themselves were chiefly concerned with a petty, though bitter quarrel over the disposition of the scanty plunder they had taken from their victims, and general recriminations against each other.

Captain Jack was finally conceded his claim to General Canby's uniform, sword and hat, with Reverend Thomas' clothes falling to Bogus and Boston Charley. Shacknasty Jim, Schonchin John and Barncho compromised by dividing Meacham's clothing among themselves.

Hooker Jim was made the object of great scorn for not killing Dyer, and bitter reproaches were leveled at Curly Head Doctor for bungling their attempt to kill Colonel Mason. But these petty quarrels gave way to preparations to defend themselves against the attack they felt was certain, and the necessity of standing together against the enemy.

Curly Head Doctor called the braves together and prepared for a great war dance. All night long the sound of weird chanting and the reverberation of drums echoed throughout the caverns surrounding their hideout, yet every nerve was tensed against the possibility of a sentinel's call, "The soldiers are coming!" When morning dawned after a sleepless night, and still no blue-coats had appeared, the Modocs were exuberant. "Soldier mans scared!" they exulted. "We show them Modoc heart, they 'fraid. Now they give us our Lost river country!"

The grave-faced Chief and Scarface Charley did not share this view of conditions. "Soldiers come, all right," they told the others. "We no scare them. Now they mad, we have to fight 'til every Modoc brave is dead!"

The day dragged on leaden feet for Captain Jack and the few who were loyal to him. He allowed neither himself nor them, any illusions as to what the result of their bloody deeds would be. Calm, though desperate, he resolved to fight to the last breath. He reminded his people that the hated Warm Spring Indians were coming to help the white men exterminate them; that the soldiers now had big guns that would bring death into the stronghold without a bluecoat coming near.

At last the shadow of Van Bremer's mountain heralded the coming of another night, and the medicine man again held sway around the fire, as he worked the spirits of his followers up to fighting pitch. He promised that his medicine would turn the biggest bullets of the palefaced enemy, pointing to the battle in the fog to prove his words. He played upon their superstitious beliefs to the point where many of them were actually convinced that they were immune to death. The white men were already conquered in their minds, and that night's war dance took on the joyous abandonment of a celebration of victory.

While the Modocs were thus engaged, seventy-two long-awaited Warm Spring Indians were dismounting from their horses at Colonel Mason's camp after a long journey from the north. Their leader, veteran of many Indian wars, reported to Colonel Mason who immediately issued orders for their accommodation.

This scout, Donald McKay, was not a Warm Spring Indian by blood, his father being a white man and his mother a Cayuse woman. Yet these Indians had the utmost confidence in him, for they had fought under his leadership on the government's side in the "Snake campaign" and they knew his caliber.

McKay had sent a messenger on ahead earlier in the day to advise General Gillem that the Warm Springs Indians would arrive that night. On receipt of the information, a feverish activity swept through the aroused military encampments as everything was made ready for the attack on the Modoc stronghold next day, the fourteenth of April. Food for the fighting forces was packed, ready to be sent forward as needed; officers went into conference to outline the plan of assault; the hospital was placed in order and even shallow graves were dug.

Groups of troopers talked in low tones, recounting their former experiences in the Lava Beds to the new-comers. Those who had known the hell of that futile January battle shrank from the thought of again en-countering such odds. Those who had been more re-cently added to the forces tried to laugh at the drawn and anxious faces of their comrades, but found it hard to shake off that feeling of strained apprehension which poisoned the very air.

Late that night the officers gathered in Colonel Green's quarters to indulge in the half-sentimental, half-solemn ceremonies that often preceded an en-gagement, and served the same purpose for the white men as a war dance did for the Indians. Although somewhat different in design, the intention of both was the same.

The recalling of brave deeds, the exchange of per-sonal friendships, the blotting out of all individual differences in the face of demands for whole-hearted action . . . these and a pledge of faithfulness to duty, even if it meant death, were the threads of the talk which was carried on in Colonel Green's tent that night.

Here were men who were going forward at break of day to meet an enemy protected by almost impregnable caverns and rocks. The chances that they would come back alive were unpredictable. Yet just before the group disbanded the officers raised their voices in a song both melancholy and daring.

> "Then stand by your glasses steady,
> This world's a round of lies;
> Three cheers for the dead already,
> And hurrah for the next who dies!"

CHAPTER XIV

STORMING THE STRONGHOLD

GRIM shadows of men began to move about the soldiers' camp at four o'clock in the morning on Monday, April 14. In the dim light, phantom-like mules stood patiently as they were packed with cannon and shells for bombarding the stronghold; food and kegs of water for the living; first aid supplies and stretchers for the dead and wounded.

Before daylight, nearly a thousand soldiers and seventy-two Warm Spring Indians were mustered silently into line, ready to move forward across the broken and scarred lava field in a massed attack on their stubborn enemy. They were unsupported this time by the steak-eating volunteers who were engaged in guarding the settlements of the valley to the north, against possible Modoc depredations.

Silent as these preparations were, the Modocs were kept informed of them through their scouts who missed not even a single movement the army made. With equal secrecy, Captain Jack ordered the old women and children of the tribe aroused from their sleep, and herded for protection far back into the deeper caves which honey-combed the stronghold. The younger squaws, who for days had been busy moulding quantities of cartridges captured in previous battle into bullets that would fit the old muskets, with which most of the Modoc warriors were equipped, were now detailed to keep the fighters supplied with water and ammunition.

As daybreak drew nearer, the braves wrapped their legs with strips of rawhide to protect them from wild gooseberry bushes and sharp-edged rocks. Many of them were armed with bright new Springfield rifles, which they carried as proud mementos of their former victory over the palefaces. Silently they slipped forward from rock to rock and crevice to crevice, until they reached the outer edge of the rampart of volcanic debris which surrounded their stronghold. There, they took position in small parapets formed in part by nature and in part by the work of their own hands in piling rock upon rock to form a loop-holed defense. Once in position, their dark-skinned bodies blended perfectly with their natural surroundings, making them indistinguishable except to the sharpest eye.

In the darkness the artillery detachments advanced toward a rocky promontory which had been selected as a base for cannon operations. It was necessary to take a circuitous route in order to find a trail smooth enough for the pack train, bearing the howitzers, to follow. There the mules were unpacked, the mounted pieces set up and trained on the Modoc stronghold. Soon all was in readiness.

A signal rocket from the station on the bluff seared through the chill, half-lighted air. Instantly the cannon roared out and the infantry advanced as rapidly as the jagged barriers of rocks and fissures would permit. In their ears thundered the reports of the howitzers which reverberated through the caverns of the region to their utmost recesses, even causing the rocks themselves to vibrate and leaving the air pungent with the smell of gunpowder.

Nearly an hour passed as the troops, spread out in a long line extending from the lake shore, a mile or so into the Lava Beds, moved cautiously forward without sighting a Modoc. The center of the line was almost upon the outer defenses of the stronghold when the bugle rang out the call to charge.

Throwing caution to the winds, running upright, the soldiers surged forward. With each step, the movement gathered momentum and daring, until of a sudden a barrage of bullets, as terrifying as it was deadly, swept the ranks, dropping one man after another. Frantically the troopers tried to locate the source of the firing, but all they could see were faint wisps of smoke rising from the rocks ahead. No human target appeared on which to train their rifles. There was nothing . . . nothing but rocks and sagebrush, smoke and noise.

Nevertheless, the soldiers directed their fire into the rocks before them. A roar of musketry swept along the line from end to end, while the shells continued to whistle through the air overhead. Officers shouted, exhorted, as the troops sought the protection of rocks or dropped where they stood . . . Modoc bullets having found their marks. "Forward!" they cried. "Let's go, boys! After 'em!"

The men responded, but from those uncanny spurts of smoke among the rocks whizzed bullets aimed with deadly accuracy. They never seemed to miss. So rapidly did one bluecoat after another fall that the thinned line soon broke. The bugle sounded retreat.

Dragging, carrying, supporting what dead and wounded they could, the soldiers fell back. On mule stretchers by land, in boats by water, the injured, groaning and cursing their luck . . . and many who would never groan or curse again . . . were carried back to camp.

Beyond range of the redskins' rifles, the soldiers entrenched themselves, threw up rock breastworks for protection where natural fortifications weren't available, and waited further orders.

After a brief rest another offensive movement was launched. Firing on both sides was furious and gradually the north end of the line made some headway. But the center ranks, confronted by a flat, almost level area nearly six hundred yards wide directly west of the stronghold, were repulsed time after time.

By nightfall, the troops had gained little advantage, but the officers were determined to hold what they had. Reinforcements were ordered up to hold the line during the night, while those who had borne the brunt of the fighting during the day straggled back to camp, their hands and knees lacerated and bloody from crawling over the rocks, their arms and faces scratched with gooseberry thorns.

On reporting to have their minor injuries dressed, they found the hospital fast filling with the wounded. While they were inside of the tent, their ragged nerves were startled by the sound of shots within the camp itself.

"What!" exclaimed the soldiers. "Are the bloody Modocs takin' the bloomin' camp?"

"Don't get excited," a steward responded gloomily. "They're just buryin' the dead."

Tense, silent, wounded and well men alike, listened while five volleys of shots boomed a last farewell to comrades less fortunate than they.

The falling of darkness brought no cessation of hostilities, although the firing became more sporadic. At irregular intervals shots cracked and echoed through the rocks, allowing little sleep to any one, and none at all to the cramped men lying on the sharp rocks, among which not even rest was possible. Cold crept numbingly over their bodies, mosquitoes buzzed and bit, cuts and scratches stung out of all proportion to their size . . . and if they dared to move to a more comfortable position a Modoc bullet, as likely as not, would spang against a rock and shatter it in their faces, always with the risk that it might make a direct hit.

With the coming of daylight, the attack was renewed full force. Forward and back the line of battle surged until the troopers began to feel they had never known anything but this pock-pitted purgatory. One shell after another continued to fall among the rocks of the stronghold with a mighty crash, sending flying fragments in every direction, yet never seeming to get the exact range of the concealed Modoc warriors. Every advance was followed by the inevitable repulse, as hidden marksmen, unseen by their enemy, continued to take their toll of life.

As the day wore on, the necessity of taking the open flat that separated the center of the line from the outposts of the stronghold became more and more imperative, if their fighting was not to be in vain. This was hazardous in the extreme, for it was directly commanded by the Modoc parapets, but offered no protection whatever to those attempting to take and hold it. Lieutenant Eagan's company was ordered up to try to accomplish the feat.

Knowing the risk involved, but daring anything, the intrepid Eagan called on his men to give their best.

"Come on, boys; it's up to us! Get your Modoc and keep on going!" he shouted as the men charged, leaping from rock to rock.

But the Modocs were not caught napping. A withering fire covered the attackers and the gallant Eagan crumpled before it, as first one soldier and then another dropped.

"Fall back!" commanded Eagan, teeth clenched as he writhed on the ground. Routed, the soldiers crouched and leapt, shouting and cursing as they retreated, leaving their officer where he lay. Entrenched once more behind protecting rocks, they covered Eagan with their guns to prevent his capture by the redskins.

Dr. Cabaniss was hastily called. He seemed to bear a charmed life, for he ducked and dodged in safety to the spot where Eagan lay convulsed with pain. A shout went up from the soldiers as Dr. Cabaniss leaned over their commander and dressed his injuries. Unable to carry the man, Cabaniss piled a few rocks between his body and the Modocs, then taking his own life in his hands, returned to the lines unscathed.

During the remainder of an exhausting day, firing was continuous, but the soldiers were cheered by a definite victory on one sector of the line. In a terrific battle which raged for nearly two hours in the late afternoon, the troops nearest the lake succeeded in executing a flank movement which connected the forces on the west of the stronghold with Colonel Mason's on the east . . . a distinct advantage, although it cost many lives, for it cut the Modocs off from their supply of water. The nearness of the soldiers to the stronghold, however, put a stop to the use of the cannon bombardment. Along the rest of the line, the Modocs held off every threat, preventing the troopers from gaining an inch.

When night fell after the second day of siege on the stronghold, the soldiers again entrenched themselves in their positions, and took advantage of the darkness to retrieve their injured comrades, among whom was Eagan. He was carried by stretcher to the hospital tent, which was now overflowing and vocalized by the groans and shrieks of men, tortured with pain. As the surgeon probed Eagan's wounds, he laughed and joked with the attendants as if he had no more than stubbed his toe.

"They use powder that couldn't even push a bullet clear through my leg!" he exclaimed, sarcastically.

But if the troops were suffering heavy casualties, the Modocs were having difficulties almost as serious. No deaths or even critical injuries had been sustained during the two days of battle, but such continuous firing was beginning to make alarming inroads into their supply of ammunition, never plentiful at best. Moreover, they had no supply of water on hand, and without it, they would be greatly handicapped the next day. The Modocs determined, therefore, to make a strenuous effort to open up a passage to the lake, at all costs, only a few hundred yards distant.

Choosing to make their attempt at night, they camouflaged themselves with sagebrush and crept slowly forward. But the soldiers had anticipated just such a move and opened on them with a scathing fire. The redskins returned it. They whooped and yelled and pushed their attack in deadly earnest. The troopers massed to resist, forced the Modocs back, but not for long. The line stiffened, moved forward again, only to have the bluecoats refuse to fall back. All night long the air rang with peal after peal, volley after volley, as one side and then the other gained an advantage.

By morning both sides suffered from fatigue to the point of exhaustion. For two days and nights the Indians had fought with practically no opportunity to rest, while the soldiers had been able to get very little. But, although the Modocs gave up their attempt to reach the lake. With the coming of dawn, there was still no sign that they were ready to surrender.

During this night of almost continuous bombardment, the casualties were heavy. Early in the morning every available pack-horse and mule-team was pressed into service, carrying in the dead and wounded. Most of these outfits belonged to private citizens, and were hired by the government for hauling supplies with no expectation that their burdens would be mangled and bleeding human freight.

But the need was imperative and the citizen-teamsters were ordered onto the battle field to salvage what life and property they could. Mule-stretchers were rigged up for the purpose, made of stout poles about twenty feet long with a canvas stretched between them. Sturdy leather straps attached to the ends of the poles were thrown over the saddles of the mules, one of which was ten feet or more in front of the other. This provided a fairly efficient, but not too comfortable means of conveying the wounded from the battle field to the hospital.

Among the men engaged in rescuing the injured and

transporting the dead in this manner, was a nineteen-
year-old boy, Eugene Hovey, whose blond head could
be seen bobbing up here and there among the boulders
as he plied back and forth with load after load of battered troopers. He took pride in the efficiency with
which he had trained his mules to this duty. From the
officers he won high commendation and from the soldiers a deep gratitude for his dependable service.

On this particular morning, Hovey had a "hunch".
Apprehension filled him with dread, and he applied to
the quartermaster for relief from stretcher duty. He
told the officer that, although he had encountered no
trouble heretofore, he seemed to be forewarned that
disaster would overcome him if he went out that day.

The quartermaster was sympathetic, but thought his
fears ungrounded and urged him to go on, compli-
menting him highly on his work. Too brave to refuse,
Hovey harnessed his mules and prepared to set out, although no law could have compelled him to go. Before
he left, he turned over his watch and valuables to a
friend, even writing a note to each of his family in case
he should not return. The friend laughed at his fears
but Hovey was grave.

"It's no joking matter," Hovey told him. "When I
have a hunch, I'm a fool not to follow it. I'm dead
certain something terrible's going to happen today."

Accompanied by only one assistant, young Hovey got
his four mules and two stretchers under way. He was
not permitted so much as a guard, for according to the
official report, "the Modocs are surrounded and cannot
escape." Moreover, other horse stretchers had been
stumbling back and forth over the rough trail without
mishap.

No one had observed several Modoc braves, led by

Hooker Jim, stealthily slipping away from the stronghold through the gap in the lines on the south. Undetected, they crept noiselessly toward the military camp at the foot of the bluff.

The two young teamsters were just opposite the site of the peace commission massacre, when a rifle cracked without warning and a bullet struck young Hovey in the head, crumpling him instantly to the ground. His companion ran as if he had been shot from the mouth of a cannon, while the bullet Hooker Jim sent whistling after him, missed.

The Indians, their savagry gaining the upper hand, vented all their pent-up hatred of the white man on Hovey. They rushed on him while still alive, scalped him, stripped him of his clothing and gun, then crushed his head beyond recognition with huge rocks.

But this was just a sideplay to Hooker Jim and his braves, whose plan was to attack the military encampment, while all the able-bodied soldiers were in the field, with the intention of capturing the supplies of ammunition which the Modocs were beginning to need so desperately.

Their approach remained unnoticed until the attention of the lieutenant in charge of the camp was caught by a slight movement among the rocks. On training his field glasses on it, he made certain that it was caused by Indians, then he immediately signalled to Colonel Green in the field, "Modocs out of stronghold and attacking camp." Acting swiftly, the lieutenant armed all the available civilians, and even some of those with more minor injuries, and prepared for defense.

The Indians knew they must act quickly, and in a matter of a few minutes, they sent a volley of lead whistling into the camp among the tents. Shot was returned for shot, but the Modocs moved steadily closer, dodging from rock to rock.

Desperately the defenders prayed for help from the soldiers in the field and as desperately stuck to their guns. The moment was tense, critical, as the raiding party inched closer and closer.

Just as it seemed inevitable that the Indians would take the camp, the hard-pressed men gave a cheer as a detachment of reserves from the Lava Beds came running toward the camp as fast as the uneven footing would permit. The attackers saw them, too, and fell back without having accomplished their purpose, to disappear among the surrounding rocks, making their way back to the stronghold empty handed.

Meanwhile fighting on the front line continued. The Modocs, becoming more and more desperate from thirst, tried the ruse of sending two or three old women to the lake for water. The soldiers were taken in at first, and held their fire to let them pass. One of the "women", however, created suspicion among the troopers. There was something about the bearing, the walk, that didn't harmonize with the woman's clothes.

"That's a man!" shouted two or three almost simultaneously.

The Indian in question broke into a run, but he was brought to a halt by a dozen rifles, the bullets having found their mark. On rolling their victim over, they saw that he was one of the younger braves whom they had never seen before. Inside of five minutes, a half dozen pieces of scalp, inexpertly carved from his head, were in possession of the soldiers. These bits of flesh and hair were divided, again and again among their comrades, until by the time they were relieved at sundown by the reserves, a score of troopers were proudly displaying a trophy from the one redskin who had been shot.

On their way back to camp, however, they passed several orderlies escorting the mangled body of young Hovey to headquarters on one of his own mule-stretchers, and their boasting stopped abruptly as they saw that *his* scalp was in possession of the Modocs. Hovey's friends, saddened and appalled over his death, prepared a coffin for him. Among the repeated volleys of musketry at the cemetery that evening, the one fired for Hovey was of special significance.

As the third night of fighting drew near, the officers held a conference to take stock of the situation. They had been able to block the Indians' access to the lake, depriving them of water, but outside of that they could report little progress, for Captain Jack and his braves had stubbornly held the flat against the attacks made upon it.

Their own heavy casualties made them averse to prolonging the fighting so they determined to mass all their forces for an early morning attack next day. Surely, they thought, Captain Jack's few warriors must, by now, be so fatigued by the unrelieved fighting that they would offer no serious resistance.

All that night the trail to the lake was carefully guarded, and a continuous light bombardment directed at the stronghold with the intention of preventing the Modocs from getting any rest. Occasionally their bullets drew fire from the redskins, but they noticed that it was only when there was an obvious target for the Modoc guns, not a shot being wasted.

At daybreak every soldier able to carry a rifle, was in the fighting line. Lying low behind the rocky fortifications they had built for themselves or captured from the enemy, they tensely awaited the order to advance.

As they lay flat on their faces among the rocks, one soldier remarked to another. "What's up with those Injuns, I'd like t' know. It's too goll-durned quiet to mean any good."

"They must be up to something," another chimed in. "Or else they're so tuckered out by now they're all sound asleep!"

"No such luck! By the jeeminy, this dead quiet's beginnin' to give me the fidgets!"

Just then the clear, silvery notes of the bugle echoed from one rocky fastness to another, and the charge was on. Every man leapt to his feet and ran forward, his gun ready for instant use. Each moment they expected to be met with a volley of Modoc lead, as they clambered over the sharp rocks, down into crevices, up the other side, stumbling, picking themselves up and plunging on. Over one terrace of volcanic terrain they went, and then another. Still no Modoc war whoop, still no barking guns.

Fear began to eat into the consciousness of the men. "We're being trapped!" one shouted, and slowed his pace. Another cursed, as he stumbled and dropped his gun. It fell into a deep crack in the rocks and he was unable to reach it. The troops were closer to the center of the stronghold now than they had ever been, and the farther they advanced the more incredibly rough the footing became.

"It's an ambush! They're going to get us where they want us and then let loose hell!" a private yelled.

"Shut up, you!" an officer barked. "We're goin' to get those Injuns this time if we have to go through two hells!"

The lines converged toward a common center with-

out a shot being fired. When the cordon closed, the
soldiers found themselves open-mouthed at a deserted
stronghold. No Modoc challenged their right to be
there, no redskin came forward in surrender.

Crestfallen and profane at their hollow victory, the
realization slowly forced itself upon them that Captain
Jack, under cover of darkness, had withdrawn his people, and was now hiding in God-only-knew what caves
and fissures in that Titan-ripped terrain.

CHAPTER XV

DEATH AT BLACK LEDGE

AT last the forces of the United States army were in the stronghold around which their activities had centered for so long. The soldiers lost no time in exploring every nook and cranny of it, partly in the hope that they would still find Captain Jack and his braves at bay in some remote recess and partly out of sheer curiosity.

They found any number of caves, some large, some small, but all showing that they had been lived in. Bones of beef the Indians had obtained from raids on the settlers were seen everywhere, as well as old guns discarded in favor of new ones taken from the white men, pieces of tule matting on which they slept, parts of soldiers' uniforms and scraps of worn leather which once formed moccasins for their feet.

In the center of a small, somewhat level clearing the embers of what had been a fire still glowed underneath. This had obviously been their council fire . . . the scene of war-dances, medicine-making and celebrations of victory. A short distance from the center of camp life, some of the soldiers located what had been the Indians' "corral", a deep gorge covered with sparse grass on the bottom. Into it ran a single trail which could easily be blocked at the top by rolling huge boulders across it, effectively preventing the escape of horses or cattle kept there.

Far back in one of the caves, a group of troopers came upon one old man and two old squaws, so decrepit that the Modocs had been forced to abandon them in their evacuation of the stronghold. The terrified old people were dragged forth into the light where their wails and moans brought other soldiers on the run.

"That's Schonchin John . . . the devil that nearly got Meacham!" shouted one of them.

"Let's give him some of his own medicine!"

"It's him, all right! Let 'im have it!"

A sort of mob frenzy swept over the troopers. Several leveled their guns at the old man and the two helpless old squaws and fired. The women were left where they lay, but the men fought for a chance to carve pieces of scalp from the head of the alleged Schonchin John . . . souvenirs to take back to the wounded peace commissioner who was still hovering between life and death.

The desire for revenge among the soldiers, however, was not satisfied with mere scalping. The old man was beheaded. As the severed head rolled from the body, one of the soldiers gave it a kick. Then others joined, using it as they would use a soccer ball.

Only the interference of one of the surgeons saved the head from complete destruction. He berated the soldiers with a fiery tongue-lashing for their savage behavior, and took the head to camp where he preserved in alcohol what was left of it. When the soldiers who participated in this orgy came to their senses, most of them felt humiliated and chagrined at the very thought of what they had done, especially when they learned that Winema and Frank Riddle had positively identified the head and established the fact that the Indian was not Schonchin John.

The regulars were soon ordered back to the military encampment with the Warm Spring scouts detailed to remain in the stronghold to prevent the Modocs from re-occupying it. Immediately, scouting parties were sent out to track down the escaped renegades, but they came back without any news. A vigilant watch from the signal station likewise failed to disclose a wisp of smoke or any other clue to their location.

The whole discouraging campaign against the Modocs would have seemed like a bad dream, except for the reality of the scores of groaning men in the hospital and the fresh mounds in the cemetery which numbered more than all of the Modoc band together. All in all, the military forces seemed in a worse predicament than ever for their ranks were depleted, their morale shattered and their enemy nowhere to be found.

Neither did the reports of public reaction, which drifted into camp from the outside world, help matters any. From Washington came a telegram urging the general to "make the attack (on the Modocs) so strong and persistent that their fate will be commensurate with their crime. You will be fully justified in their utter extermination."

That word "extermination", had become a byword throughout the country. It glared from banner lines of newspapers, which reported it was advocated by everyone from national and state legislators to the commonest man on the street. In the editorial columns of newspapers, everything from long-range sharp-shooters to steel armor for the soldiers, and even bloodhounds and sulphur smoke was advocated as exterminating means, by those who thought they knew all about how to combat the Modocs. To them the reverses of the army were incredible.

Indeed the reverses were incredible even to the army itself, and the morale of the men was at an extremely low ebb when a more or less trivial incident sent it still lower. Several days after the empty victory at the stronghold, about fourteen Modoc braves who had slipped away from their hideout to get water at the lake, deliberately "thumbed their noses" at the army by making a mock attack upon the camp.

They took up a position not more than eight hundred yards from headquarters and challenged the soldiers to "come and get 'em". A company was immediately dispatched to bring them in. There was a rattle of musket fire, punctuated with Modoc war whoops, then the soldiers were seen returning to camp pell-mell. Captain Ferree, standing in the door of the hospital tent, relayed the story to Meacham, within.

"Here they come minus three men!" he exclaimed. "But the Modocs are following up! Doesn't that beat the Devil and the Dutch? You've seen a big dog chase a coyote until the coyote turns on him, haven't you . . . then turn tail and run for home with the coyote after him? Well, that's exactly what's happening out there now. This beats anything I ever saw, by Jupiter! Two to one, the Modocs take the camp!"

Ferree glanced at Meacham and started to chuckle. "By gorry, old man, don't know what we'll do with you if they do! You can't run, can't fight and you're too banged up to carry. Wish I had a spade, I'd bury you until the fun's over. But it's too late! Can't help it, old man. You needn't dodge, it wouldn't do any good. Just lie still and play dead on 'em again. You can do that to perfection. And there ain't a darned bit of danger that they'll try to get another scalp off of you. Too much prairie above the timber line for that! Boson Charley was a darned fool to try it before!"

Meacham smiled at Ferree's good-natured banter and listened apprehensively as occasional shots fell among the tents near where he lay.

"They're still comin'! By cracky, we'll have fun now! They're getting ready to shell 'em. Ha! Shell a dozen Modocs! Don't that beat Sulphur King out of his boots? They're goin' to fire. Steady, old man, steady now. Keep cool. Yip-se-lanta! There it goes, screechin', screamin' right in among the rocks where the Injuns are. And did it explode!"

When the smoke cleared away, however, every one of the Indians popped up from behind the rocks where they had taken refuge and insolently patted their shot pounches at the "Bosteena soldiers". Time after time this happened, the Modocs taking to cover until the shell exploded, then strutting out to make mocking gestures at the army men.

It was a waste of shells. "Cease firing!" ordered General Gillem, and then the cannons were covered with their neat canvas housings.

Within plain sight, the Modocs then organized a mock artillery battery. Obviously contemptuous, they elevated their rifles at an angle imitating the shell guns, and at an order from Scarface Charley, who stood behind, swept the unprotected camp with shots that spit down dangerously near the hospital and other tents.

By that time, enough soldiers had been mustered to make the Modoc position untenable and they soon dropped back toward the lake, from which they returned to their hidden camp by such a round-about way that the soldiers were still left in the dark as to its whereabouts.

As things quieted down a little, Captain Fairchild appeared at the tent door and greeted Ferree. "I say, Cap'n, don't you wish we had them volunteers here now? A fine chance they'd have had for some of them Modoc steaks they was hankerin' for! They're the fellows that could take in the Modocs! But where in the devil are the Warm Springs all this time?"

"Warm Springs?" Ferree grinned. "They're out on the other side of the lavas surrounding the Modocs to keep 'em from gettin' away!"

"They ain't goin' to leave here very soon," Fairchild predicted. "But did you ever see anything like this morning's performance? Fourteen Indians come out, kill three men, threaten the camp, scare everybody to death and then retire in glory to their own camp without our men even learnin' where it is! That caps the climax. Them Modocs is mighty devilish fellers, an' it'd be just like 'em to attack the camp en masse . . . and if they did, they'd take it sure!"

As Fairchild and Ferree sauntered off together, Lieutenant Tom Wright stopped in for a chat with Meacham. "Say, them Modocs are just about hell!" he burst out.

Meacham taunted him good-naturedly. "Where are your two thousand dollars now? I suppose you and Eagan still think you can take 'em in fifteen minutes, eh?"

"Take 'em, not much!" Wright growled. "The only thing we took was the worst beatin' ever an army got in the world!"

"Pretty mean place, the stronghold?"

"It's no use talkin'. The match to the Modoc stronghold's never been built and never will be. Give me a hundred picked men and let me station 'em and I could hold that place against five thousand. Yes, ten thousand. If them redskins hadn't run out of water and maybe ammunition, we'd never got 'em outa there. I'm tellin' you it's the most impregnable fortress in the world. Sumpter ain't no where in comparison!"

Meacham enjoyed drawing Wright out. "And what about Captain Jack?" he queried.

"Captain Jack? Why, he's the biggest Injun on the continent! Look what he's done! Licked near a thousand men, killed upwards of fifty and not lost more than two or three himself. We starved him out. We didn't whip 'im. He'll turn up in a day or two spoilin' for another fight. I tell you, Jack's a heap big Injun!"

Such sentiments as these were common talk as one day of inactivity followed another with each sunset gun booming a farewell to many of the wounded whose injuries proved fatal. On the afternoon of April 25, however, nine days after the battle, the signal station reported locating smoke coming from the vicinity of a low butte some five or six miles distant in the midst of the Lava Beds.

That night General Gillem determined to send out a new scouting party for the purpose of determining the exact location of the Modoc position and whether or not cannon could be placed within range of it. He summoned Captain E. Thomas, placed him in charge of the expedition and instructed him to go as far south as Black Ledge. Fourteen Warm Springs scouts under Donald McKay would be ordered to leave the stronghold and meet him en route. Under no circumstances was he to provoke an attack by the Indians.

Early the next morning, there was an unusual bustle about camp as preparations were made for the departure of the scouting party which was composed of sixty-six regulars, five officers, three packers, a surgeon and a civilian guide . . . seventy-six men in all. Guns were inspected, ammunition distributed, mules packed with food, water and medical supplies.

The soldiers were cheerful as they left camp, for activity seemed good after so much waiting. The whole affair at first struck them as a Sunday picnic rather than serious business. But when they reached the region where the country became more rugged, their ardor was tempered by uneasiness characterized by watchful scrutiny of their surroundings. Every defile they must traverse held the possibility of attack from ambush; every rocky terrace became a potential screen for lurking redskins. Even the swift, darting movements of ground squirrels were enough to keep the soldiers' fingers close to their triggers.

"Wonder what's keepin' those Warm Springs?" one of the men remarked. "They should've come up with us before now."

"Well, when they do, here's hopin' they give us plenty of warnin' or they're likely to find themselves full of lead before they know what's happened. They look too durned much like them Modocs fer comfort!" another replied.

They had stumbled along for what seemed to them an eternity, over footing that was bad enough, when they came face to face with a tongue of broken lava which had flowed out across the older formations at the time this purgatory was being formed. It was a jumbled, sharp-edged pile of volcanic debris, covering quite an extensive area on which no vegetation could find a foothold.

"Great guns! How's that for the devil's golf-course!" exclaimed Thomas. "If we try to cross it, we won't have any soles on our boots or skin on our hands inside of ten minutes. Guess we'll have to detour." He issued orders to that effect.

It took considerable time to skirt the edge of this lava flow, and four hours had passed, making it nearly noon, before they had covered the five miles to the foot of Black Ledge. They found it similar in surroundings to Captain Jack's stronghold . . . a pitted, boulder-strewn wilderness of irregular chasms, terraces and sagebrush.

Thomas located one spot, however, in a comparatively large depression, where the ground was level enough for the men to sit down in comfort and here he called a halt.

"Funny about those Warm Springs," he commented, a note of anxiety in his voice. Then he laughed. "Well, anyway, we haven't seen any Modocs! Find yourselves a good resting place and we'll bivouac for an hour."

The men, tired and hungry, needed no urging. They stacked their guns and sprawled on the ground as comfortably as possible. Some of them took off their boots to ease their tired feet, while others searched their clothing for wood ticks which had clung to them and were beginning to bore in.

Once more they were in a good-humor, the fear of a Modoc attack having abated considerably with their safe arrival at their destination. There was the usual banter, laughter and conversational tid-bits as they started to make short work of the food the packers laid out.

A noticeable change began to come over them, however, as they became aware of a peculiar stillness which hung over everything like a pall. Not even the chirp of a bird broke the uncanny silence. It even seemed that the surrounding rocks caught up their voices, making them sound hollow and turning their laughter into noisy mockery.

Lieutenant Cranston became restless and uneasy. "When you don't see any Indians is just the time to look out for 'em," he observed. "I'm going to scout around and see what's over that ridge, there. Who's with me?"

Twelve men responded and together they left their comrades and headed for the rocky embankment nearby. No sooner had they disappeared over its crest than a bedlam of Modoc warwhoops shrilled through the silence and brought every man to his feet. Leaden bullets spatted among them like hail. Before they could make a move, a half dozen men had fallen, among them Lieutenant Howe. Panic seized them and many plunged headlong for the protection of the rocks, without coats, boots or guns. Others fought their own comrades in a grand scramble to secure a weapon from the dog pile that developed around the stacked rifles.

Thomas tried to rally his men. "Might as well die here as anywhere!" he shouted. "Come on, men, we'll lick the tar out of 'em."

Rifles barked, officers shouted, Indians whooped, men cried out as they were bored by bullets. "Take position on that side hill!" yelled Thomas above the din to Lieutenant Harris, who, with his men, attempted to carry out the order. But the Modocs were still higher and fired down among them until they were forced back, leaving two dead and one wounded behind them. In the retreat, Harris himself was fatally shot.

One after another the five officers were picked off with unerring precision. The next victim to fall to the Modoc marksmen with a bullet through his head was Thomas. Lieutenant Wright, with four leads lodged in his body dragged himself into a crevice, and found three of his men, all wounded, there before him. He died in their arms as one of them tried to pour water from a canteen between his clenched teeth. Cranston and the twelve men with him had walked into a barrage of lead and in less than a minute every one of their bodies lay in a veritable shambles at the foot of the ledge over which they had gone.

The fissures into which most of the unarmed troopers had crawled now became death traps as the Modocs closed in to complete their slaughter. Every helpless soldier they could find was shot and scalped, while the redskins quarreled with each other in their eagerness to see who could obtain the most plunder. Guns and ammunition were their primary concern, but canteens, boots, hats and even whole uniforms were taken.

While this was going on, those troopers who still had life in their bodies could not believe their ears as they heard a voice, recognized by some of the soldiers as that of Scarface Charley, cry out, "All you mans what ain't dead better go home! We don't want to kill you all in one day!" At a command from their leader, the Modocs withdrew, leaving a bloody slaughter scene behind them.

They had not been gone fifteen minutes when the Warm Springs appeared . . . too late! They did what little they could to ease the suffering of the wounded and then set off as fast as they could go to carry the tragic news to headquarters.

Despairing of rescue, the wounded lay there, wracked with pain, tortured with thirst, haunted by fear. The cold, jagged lava rocks yielded no rest, making movement an agony. Yet the urge to live was so strong that when dusk came to give protection, those who could tried to crawl on hands and knees toward camp.

At headquarters an appalled General Gillem listened to the Warm Springs' account of what they had seen, and he issued orders immediately for the formation of a rescue party. In less than a half hour after the news was received, several detachments of soldiers were moving in two lines across the lava field in the direction of Black Ledge. As darkness gathered, a huge fire was built on the bluff above the military encampment to guide any who had been fortunate enough to survive the massacre.

Even nature, it seemed, was working against the white men, for the coming of night brought with it a driving storm. The rescue party became numbed, not only with the cold, but with the thought of what their injured comrades must be suffering from exposure to the elements in addition to their wounds.

The Warm Springs scouts acted as guides for the rescuers, but, as the blackness became more and more opaque, they finally had to admit that they had lost their sense of direction. There was nothing to do but camp and wait for daylight. With hands that ached with cold and hearts leaden with anxiety, the soldiers piled up rocks as best they could to protect themselves both from the biting wind and a possible Indian attack. They could not, they dare not sleep.

About midnight they were startled into alertness by

sounds they thought sure was the approach of Modoc prowlers. Tensely they waited with ears strained as the sounds grew closer. The guard called out the challenge, "Who goes there?"

"Eight men from Captain Thomas' detachment," came the reply.

The soldiers breathed easily once more as they gathered around the exhausted troopers, six of whom were wounded. The two uninjured men offered to guide the rescue party to the charnel house at Black Ledge, and the officer in charge detailed a small squad to accompany them and report back. The two guides stumbled off with the soldiers following, but with no landmarks to guide them they searched vainly for over half an hour. At last they had to return to the lines and confess they had failed.

After a seemingly endless night, the darkness gave way to streaks of dull light in the east, then two men were sent forward to try to locate the scene of the massacre. They had been gone only a few minutes when they returned and announced that they had found it within a few hundred yards of where the soldiers were camped.

Immediately the main rescue force moved forward and in the gray light of a gray morning, they came upon the slain and wounded, lying in dim crevices, under clumps of sagebrush or in the exposure of the open flat. These were men they knew . . . their comrades. Some were rigid in positions of desperate defense; some sprawled in pools of their own blood. Those who had survived the night, suffering the agony of painful wounds, cried out weakly for water, for help, as they saw their rescuers approach. On every face, dead and alive, was written the story of their terrible experience.

Quickly fires were built, water was heated and the surgeons set about dressing wounds as best they could with the emergency equipment at hand. As they worked they learned from the pallid lips of their patients that the rescue forces had been so close that the stricken men had heard the soldiers piling up rocks, had even caught the faint sound of their voices. Yet fear had held them paralyzed, for they were so imbued with the thought of redskins that they thought the sounds were those of the Modocs who had returned to finish off their job when daylight permitted. After such suspense, their relief was pathetic.

All that day was spent in treating the wounded and searching for the bodies of the dead. Finding there were too many dead bodies to bring in that night, the corpses were piled together and covered over with sagebrush grubbed from the rocks. Toward evening the bodies of the officers and a few of the regulars were lashed upon pack mules, and the wounded were made as comfortable as possible on stretchers.

As the sun sank from sight and dusk settled over the desolate wilderness of the Lava Beds, rescuers and rescued started back to camp with the Warm Spring scouts in the lead. Behind them, single file, came a long row of stretchers bearing mangled troopers, who stoically tried to stifle their groans. The six men on the handles of each litter endeavored to pick their footing carefully to spare the injured all the jarring possible. Relief crews carried the guns of the stretcher bearers, ready to take over the job when the others tired. Mules bearing the dead brought up the rear.

Only a few miles lay between them and camp, but

those miles were equal to a march of thirty or forty miles over level ground. The jumble of pock-pitted, chasm-cleft rocks became almost insurmountable barriers to those with the stretchers, but somehow they managed to make headway, slow and discouraging 'though it was. Darkness added to their difficulties for they dared not use the lanterns they had brought for fear the light would tempt the Modocs to draw down upon them.

The stretcher bearers often called for relief, for the strain of lifting the dead weight of their burdens over rocks and across gulches became unbearable. In spite of the care with which the men moved, the injured were jolted unmercifully until their cries became almost continuous. If, from some stretcher, these sounds ceased to come, the bearers knew what had happened . . . the man was dead.

Suddenly a raucous noise split through the surrounding silence and the soldiers dropped to the ground as if shot. They waited in almost unendurable suspense, trying vainly to identify the sound and fully expecting to be the target of Modoc bullets. Then the ear-splitting sound came once more . . . the wild braying of one of the mules!

Some of the soldiers were able to laugh at their fright, but it was enough to break the overwrought nerves of many of the troopers who became utterly demoralized. Frantic, they decamped from the line under cover of darkness, and plunged blindly in the direction of the beacon on the bluff, obsessed with only one idea . . . that of reaching safety. So widespread was the desertion that the stretcher bearers sought relief in vain, until finally even the officers had to pitch in and help shoulder the loads to keep the men from falling in complete exhaustion.

As a somber dawn began to break at last, the muscle-weary men were still some distance from their destination. But instead of lifting their spirits, the coming of daylight only added a new fear . . . that the Indians would now be able to locate them. Almost at the end of their physical endurance from the night-long struggle at the stretchers, they knew that in such an event they would be easy prey for the redskins. This one contingency, however, they were spared, and about eight o'clock the abject rescue party straggled into camp.

CHAPTER XVI

MODOC BLOODHOUNDS

EVERY resource of the camp was taxed to the limit in taking care of the wounded whose pallid faces were ghastly gray in the morning light and whose groans of pain were continuous. Yet in spite of the utmost exertions of the attendants in their behalf, the suffering of many of the men proved in vain as they succumbed to the fate which had taken so many of their comrades more quickly and mercifully.

The majority of the men belonging to the rescue party, also needed medical attention after their long-continued exposure and their utter exhaustion. Dark rings encircled their strangely sunken eyes, and deep-set lines marked their drawn faces.

From among the able-bodied men in camp, another detachment was drafted to go out and recover the bodies of those whom the first rescue party had been forced to leave at Black Ledge. The wrath and indignation of these soldiers leapt beyond bounds when, instead of the bodies of their comrades, they found nothing but a mound of ashes and bones, mute evidence that the Modocs had been there before them.

When the roll was called that night, it was found that only twenty-three men, less than one-third of the scouting party which had started for Black Ledge, had survived the ordeal unscathed, the other fifty-three men having been killed or seriously wounded.

The loss of so many of their comrades affected the soldiers deeply. Men who had been in the army for years and who had witnessed the horrors of the Civil war, wept without shame. Over the whole encampment hung the feeling of despondency, made still more poignant by the realization that six futile months had elapsed since the army first undertook to capture the renegade Chief . . . and, still, he was at large.

Into such an atmosphere, came General Jeff C. Davis, newly appointed Commander of the Department of the Columbia, to take over the duties of the late General Canby in directing the campaign against Captain Jack. He had not been in camp a day before he had sized up the situation and dispatched the following report to Washington:

"It (the Black Ledge massacre) proved to be one of the most disastrous affairs our army has had to record. Its effects were very visible on the morale of the command, so much so that I deemed it imprudent to order the aggresssive movements which had been my desire and intention to make at once upon my arrival."

Davis took immediate steps to prevent the attitude of defeatism from gaining a permanent hold. With dynamic vigor, this tall, angular man moved into action, his first order being to move the camp from the Lava Beds to Fairchild's ranch. This change occupied the men for several days during which their spirits rose considerably as they caught the contagion of optimism which Davis radiated. He was blunt, short-spoken, but underneath his rough manner the men came to recognize an unexpected sympathy and sense of humor which made their respect for him grow by leaps and bounds. They liked the way he moved about among them with his high-crowned, broad-brimmed hat perched at an angle on the side of his head and a carelessness in his dress which bespoke his indifference to anything that did not further the business at hand.

While the camp was being moved, Davis had the Warm Springs scouting the Lava Beds for traces of the Modocs. They reported that every evidence pointed to their having left that region and headed south toward the Pit river country. A glance at the map showed Davis that, if this were true, many innocent settlers might be made victims of the plundering renegades. He determined to forestall this possibility by immediately starting a force in pursuit of them.

Two companies of light cavalry and one of artillery were ordered out with the Warm Springs scouts as guides. On the night of May 9, they had reached the vicinity of Dry lake, some thirty-five or forty miles from Fairchild's ranch on the opposite southern extremity of the Lava Beds. Here the cavalry troops set up camp while the artillery selected a site about a mile distant in the pine timber.

Up to this time, the soldiers had seen no sign of the Modocs, but they took the routine precaution of stationing outposts on nearby bluffs. The horses were allowed free range to forage, and after the evening meal, the two military camps settled down for the night with a feeling of security.

Although the soldiers had seen no trace of the Modocs, there was not a move by the army which went unobserved by the renegade scouts. After noting every detail of the Dry lake camp, including the location of pickets, these renegade scouts returned to their tribesmen who were determined to attack their pursuers before they themselves were attacked, choosing the break of day as the best time to swoop down on the white men.

The cavalry camp was tranquil, the soldiers were peacefully sleeping, when an uproar of war-whoops and shouting caused the soldiers to spring from their blankets as if electrified. Horses stampeded through the camp, plunging and kicking. Men grabbed their guns and sought protection of the nearest shelter. One after another, four soldiers and two Warm Springs scouts staggered and fell as the Modocs pressed the attack. Six dead, seven wounded . . . and the fight had just begun!

Curt commands from officers quickly brought some degree of order out of the confusion, and the bugle rang out the call to charge. The men started forward into the barrage of Modoc bullets, then halted in their tracks with open mouths, as they caught sight of a blue-uniformed figure wearing all the trappings of an officer, stationed on the bluff from which the Modoc lead had come. They held their fire, fearing lest they kill a captured comrade.

The uniformed figure stood still for a moment, outlined against the jagged skyline, then boldly strutted back and forth before the astonished soldiery. After the first shock, the troopers suddenly understood the ruse. "It's Captain Jack in Canby's uniform!" one of them cried. "Let 'im have it!"

A taunting war-whoop from the bluff confirmed the

hoax as every soldier took aim, only to have the ghost of General Canby disappear before they could pull their triggers. Infuriated and chagrined, the soldiers charged the bluff as one man, each trooper vainly seeking to get another glimpse of that blue-uniformed figure so he could have the vengeful pleasure of riddling it with bullets.

The Modocs scattered, fell back, one redskin dropped. But the rest of the band dodged from rock to rock, pulling up sage-brush as they ran to use as a screen. So perfect was their concealment that the soldiers could see nothing at which to fire except the puffs of smoke from their rifles. For a few minutes the two forces were dead-locked, then the Modocs slowly but surely pushed the white men back. Their aims were accurate and seldom missed their targets.

The plight of the cavalry troops was becoming desperate when the artillery, which had been sent for, came up at double-quick. Seeing the reinforcements, the Indians knew it would be foolhardy to engage them in battle, and hastily retreated, deserting their ponies, whose packs jounced on their packs as they ran, frightened, among the rocks.

The troopers followed up, firing shot after shot, but no Modoc fell. From then on the battle became a foot race with the soldiers at a decided disadvantage. Yet they jumped, ran, stumbled over the rocks with a determination inflamed by Captain Jack's insult. At the end of three miles, however, they were so hopelessly outdistanced that they decided to give up the chase.

Frustrated but not despondent, the troopers started the trek back to camp, exhilerated with a sense of at least partial victory, unknown heretofore. They had killed one Modoc, captured twenty-four ponies bearing food and ammunition, and routed the redskins for the first time. For once the soldiers had not been the ones to retreat, and it bolstered their morale, despite the loss of seven of their comrades.

Couriers were immediately dispatched to headquarters with a report of the encounter, and Davis, without delay, rushed forward reinforcements numbering a hundred and seventy men. While these men were on their way, the Warm Springs scouts picked up the trail of the renegades and reported that they had fortified themselves near Sandy Butte, only six miles or so from the soldiers' Dry lake camp.

There was one thing, however, which the Warm Springs scouts did not know . . . namely, what was going on within the Modoc camp, which was the scene of harsh words and angry wranglings. The dispute was the climax of dissention which had been growing for some time and now centered on the death of Ellen's Man, the brave who had fallen victim to the soldiers' bullets.

While the troopers were preparing to push the attack on Captain Jack, the Chief himself stood stolidly, with folded arms, in the center of a circle of braves, while Bogus Charley paced up and down before him, talking and gesticulating wildly, his stentorian voice charged with the very wrath of the devil.

"What for you let Ellen's Man get killed?" Bogus demanded of Jack. "It your fault he die! You all time try to save own skin. We no fight for you no more! We done fighting for coward Chief!"

For seconds, Captain Jack fixed his penetrating eyes upon the rebellious braves in silence, while all the pent-up hate and fury of a man who finds himself betrayed, distorted his face. The sting of his glance fell chiefly on Bogus, Shacknasty Jim, Steamboat Frank, Hooker

Jim and Curly Head Doctor, each in turn. Then words leapt from his lips as from a tongue of fire, the mutinous leaders cringing before his seering scorn.

"You yellow dogs! You show what you are! You come to me and whine because a man is killed. You 'fraid to die! Why you no think of that when you kill innocent settlers? Why you no think of that when you make me kill Canby? Now you cry like papoose. Always I plead with you for peace. 'Squaw! Coward!' you call me then. You put squaw clothes on me. I should have killed you instead of soldier ty-ee Canby! Him better man than all you traitors!

"Where your Curly Head Doctor man's charms now? Long as everything good, you very brave. Now when dark cloud come you run to save bird-hearted souls. All right, run! As for me, I die fighting!"

Hooker Jim, livid with rage at the tongue-lashing, raised his gun and shouted, "Kill him! Kill him!" But before he could press the trigger, William Faithful knocked the gun from his hands.

"You no kill our Chief!" William cried. "You want to shoot, there plenty soldiers left. Go use bullets on them!"

Captain Jack still faced Hooker Jim with that piercing look, not a muscle moving. "You never kill me!" he sneered. "You have heart like fish. But I tell you, Jack is no coward. Jack no die at hands of coward. Hooker Jim never kill him!"

An ominous milling surged in a wave over the rebellious braves. Equally ominous was the silence of those loyal to their Chief. They were all triggered, ready to let fly at each other with a volcanic accumulation of bitterness and hatred.

At that crucial moment, when anything might have

happened, a sentinel shouted from a rocky outpost, "Soldiers come! Soldiers come!" For the time being, their quarrel was forgotten in the necessity for defending themselves against a common enemy.

Three hundred and fifty strong that enemy attacked the Modoc position, bombarding it with shell and rifle shot, unrelentingly. A skirmish line surrounded the camp as darkness fell . . . a darkness which brought no respite. All night long, the shells continued to roar and crash like thunder, and with each passing hour the troops felt more certain that when morning came they could take the redskins without difficulty.

When the cordon of soldiers closed in at dawn, however, the eager troopers found their bombarding had been a futile waste of shells, for the Modocs were gone, having slipped silently away during the night. Stung by the irony of it, the three hundred and fifty soldiers waited in irate impatience as the Warm Spring Indians were again called into service to track down their prey.

In a short time the scouts returned with word that they had picked up a trail heading west along the old Tichnor road. The cavalry spurred their horses in pursuit and after a ride of some thirty miles, overtook the redskins, whose progress was hindered by the presence of their women and children. One glimpse of the soldiers was enough to send the braves scuttling for the brush and timber of Van Bremer's mountain, on the slopes of which a fierce running battle was waged. From their hiding places behind junipers and boulders, the Modocs shot the horses from under the soldiers, but, strangely enough, made no attempt to kill the troopers themselves.

As the shadows lengthened, the cavalrymen were forced to withdraw, having captured a few squaws, but otherwise, having done no more than exhausted themselves, their horses and their ammunition. Ruefully they headed for Fairchild's ranch, those whose horses had been shot having to cover the seven or eight miles on foot.

Davis was far from impressed with the showing the troops had made, but did not allow it to discourage him. Only his sense of humor, however, enabled him to swallow his disappointment when one of the captive squaws was induced to talk, and she told him that the band had been on its way to headquarters to surrender when they had been attacked at Van Bremer's mountain! Now, she said, they would be afraid to come in! Immediately Davis talked the situation over with John Fairchild, who agreed to go with two of the squaws to reassure the Modocs that they would be well treated if they gave themselves up.

As a result of their efforts, a cry was heard from the guards at the outposts about sundown on May 22. "Here they come!" they shouted. "They're going to surrender!" Instantly every man in camp was on the alert. Not a sound marred the expectant hush, as a long train of human wrecks and pack-animals approached. Riding in advance was Fairchild, who fixed his sharp gaze on the statuesque soldiers, thus giving orders more effective than words to let the Indians pass unharmed.

Silent as a funeral cortege, the band of seventy-five persons straggled into camp with the braves in the lead, each wearing at least some part of the United States uniform. Following them, piled on the backs of gaunt ponies, were the squaws and children, a motley crowd. Most of the clothing they wore consisted of odds and ends secured from the looting of farm houses along Tule lake after the Lost river battle. The warriors were dirty, the squaws filthy and the children could scarcely be seen for accumulated grime. Added to this, and giving the final touch of grotesqueness to their hideous appearance was the pitch they had smeared on their faces as a sign of mourning.

As the procession moved into camp, the soldiers were jubilant with the thought that at last the gruelling campaign against the Modoc renegades was at an end. They were decidedly let down, therefore, when they learned that Captain Jack and the majority of the braves were not among the captives!

The disappointed troopers were not long in learning the reason why, as the news Fairchild had gathered from talking to the Indians spread swiftly. After the escape at Sandy Butte, he said, the band had split into two factions, with the Chief and about twenty-four of the braves loyal to him going east, the rest of them west. The Warm Springs had picked up the trail of the latter and while the soldiers were following up this lead, Captain Jack had been allowed over a week in which to make good his escape.

Davis took the blow standing and swore he would get Jack if it took him all summer. He was still undecided as to what specific course to follow, however, when several of the braves, headed by Bogus Charley, appeared at his field-tent with the offer to hunt down Captain Jack and lead the soldiers to him. They said he would almost certainly be found in the vicinity of Clear lake, just over the mountains from Tule lake, where he would have plenty of water, wild game, fish and roots close at hand.

Davis was loath to accept their services, but the more he thought about it, the more it seemed to him there was much to gain and little to lose by agreeing to their proposition, even though he realized the braves were motivated by a desire to escape punishment for their part in the war. After trying them on short expeditions with the troops, he decided that if it meant bringing the campaign to a quick and successful conclusion, it would be worth any risk involved in taking advantage of their truckling spirit.

Accordingly, he arranged to have a few of the troops remain at Fairchild's ranch to hold their prisoners of war, while the rest of the headquarter's camp was moved once more . . . this time to Applegate's ranch at Clear lake. Within a few days, Bogus Charley, Shacknasty Jim, Steamboat Frank and Hooker Jim were outfitted with uniforms, army rifles, four days' provisions and Fairchild's best horses. Proud of their new acquisitions, they set off to track down their Chief for the white men.

Their surmise as to his whereabouts proved correct, for they had no trouble in locating a clearly defined trail which led east from Clear lake up the canyon of Willow creek. After following it for about fifteen miles, they came upon Captain Jack's camp and found him sitting in front of an improvised wick-i-up. As they stepped from behind some brush into full view, the Modoc Chief's smouldering eyes raked them from head to foot. He lost no detail of the army equipment, nor did his warriors who silently lined up beside him.

"What for you come?" demanded Jack. "Who send you here?"

Bogus told him all that had happened: how the rest of the band had surrendered, how well they had been treated. He advised Captain Jack and his braves to give up trying to fight the soldiers.

Incensed, the renegade Chief jumped to his feet.

"Jack no fool!" he cried. "Jack not blind! His blood boils at words you say! Your talk is crooked like snake. You cannot talk a straight talk. You buy yourselves off by leading soldiers here. But they never capture Captain Jack! Go tell them all their men are not enough to capture Kientepoos, Chief of the Modocs! And go quick, before I forget you are Modocs and kill you dead!"

Seething with anger, he stared them out of camp, but instead of leaving immediately, they hung around the outskirts where they talked to many of their friends and learned that all of them didn't feel as Captain Jack did. They were tired of hardships, tired of being always on the run and wanted to surrender.

The scouts did not stay long, however, and by noon on Wednesday, they arrived at the Applegate ranch headquarters with the report that they had located Captain Jack. By daybreak Thursday morning, the troops were on their way en masse for the Modoc camp.

When they were but a short distance away, the three companies divided, a detachment being stationed at every strategic point in the vicinity, with skirmish lines deployed to surround the renegade band. Everything was in readiness and awaiting the order to attack, when a delegation of Modoc warriors appeared and laid down their arms. Their spokesman, Boston Charley, called out, "Modocs give up! You promise your men no shoot, me go get others, they lay down guns, quit fighting."

Colonel Green, in command of the troops, agreed and the Modoc braves had started back to bring in their people when a shot rang out. It was Steamboat Frank's gun, the hammer of which had caught as he wheeled his horse. But the Modocs, who had cautiously begun to gather during the parley, thought the shot was directed at Boston Charley. Instantly they scattered and disappeared as if the canyon itself had swallowed them up.

Boston Charley assured the angry Green that, for a plug of tobacco, he would find the frightened Modocs and convince them that everything was all right. The colonel divided his own plug with the Indian and told him to assure his people that if they would come out and lay down their guns, no one would be harmed.

In order to do this, Boston Charley had to cross to the other side of the canyon. As he did so, a detachment of soldiers who knew nothing of what had happened, came up on that side and took him captive. He was sent to the rear under guard, spitting tobacco juice with gusto as he tried volubly to convince his captors of their mistake. But the more he expostulated, the more certain the soldiers became that he was trying to pull the wool over their eyes and make good his escape.

Meanwhile, Colonel Green waited impatiently for Boston Charley to return with the rest of the band. He had just about decided that it was all a clever hoax, when he learned that the Indian had been taken captive by his own men. Then he cut loose with a string of words that fairly cracked his lips, for in the meantime dusk had fallen, the Indians had slipped away and it was too late to start in pursuit. There was nothing to do but bivouac the troops for the night, their only gain being the capture of a few of the squaws and children, among them Jack's sister, Queen Mary.

At dawn the next morning, the "Modoc bloodhounds", as the soldiers called the traitor scouts, again picked up the trail of their Chief, leading up the precipitous gorge of Willow creek, then over ridges and canyons in the direction of Langell valley. The cavalry troops followed the trackers, but the footing was so difficult, even for the best trained horses, that they literally left behind them a trail of blood and horse-shoes.

Several miles south of Langell valley, the trail was lost where the fleeing Indians had taken to the rim rock. For two hours the pursuers were delayed while the scouts scattered and scoured the vicinity in every direction. At last their yells indicated they had recovered the trail and the soldiers, over two hundred in number, cheered lustily as they once more took up the chase which led them along the crest of the bluff, then down a steep trail along its side.

Suddenly four rifle shots whizzed from the rocks over the troopers' heads, followed by a shout as Scarface Charley, Schonchin John and three other Modocs stepped out from the rocks, threw down their guns and cried, "Don't shoot! We surrender!"

The five braves were escorted under guard to a spot on Lost river where the soldiers prepared to camp, for darkness was fast closing in. Scarface told them that Captain Jack and the rest of the warriors were hidden in the canyon and would probably give themselves up in the morning.

Dr. Cabaniss was determined to secure the Modoc Chief's immediate surrender, if possible, and induced Scarface Charley to take him and Queen Mary to Captain Jack's hiding place, after promising he would take no soldiers with him. They found the Chief seated on a rock in the center of a small lava field, wrapped in a faded army blanket, head buried in his hands. To Cabaniss, he seemed even more lonely than his surroundings. Queen Mary, with tears in her eyes, pleaded with him to surrender, but Captain Jack received her sullenly and he said little, except that he would give himself up next day. With that, Cabaniss had to be content.

When morning came, the troopers prepared to receive the captured Chief with a triumphal procession . . . but during the night another procession had already taken place. At its head was the obdurate Captain Jack, determined to make those who had betrayed him work for their prey . . . and their pay!

A dispatch, "Captain Jack again escapes," was forwarded to General Davis at headquarters by courier. On receiving the news, he immediately ordered a fresh detachment of cavalry into the field under Captain Perry, with instructions to head east along Willow creek to intercept Captain Jack if he should double back on his trail, which seemed likely. Several Warm Springs scouts were detailed to go in advance of the troop to be on the lookout for fresh tracks.

They had ridden for several miles parallel to the deep, rugged gorge of Willow creek, when the scouts suddenly dismounted and started to crawl about on their hands and knees. The soldiers watched with intense interest as they painstakingly inspected tracks, rocks, bushes, grass and every other object in the immediate vicinity.

Finally they pointed out to Captain Perry what they had found . . . the print of moccasins on a small mesa of pulverized lava, made in such a way as to indicate the Indian had been running. About twenty or thirty yards from this were other footprints where several Indians had passed along, each stepping in the track of the other. It was obviously a "hot" trail.

The air was cool and bracing, the horses seemed to sense the excitement of the chase as the troopers pressed eagerly forward. They had not gone far, when Captain Perry located one of the few places where it was possible to cross the box-like canyon on horseback. He divided his command and deployed the men along both banks and the two divisions moved forward opposite each other.

Shortly they were warned by signs from the scouts to make as little noise as possible. They pointed to squaw tracks leading out from, then back into the gulch. They were quite fresh. While inspecting them, Captain Perry glanced up and caught sight of something moving about a hundred yards to the left and near the top of the ravine. He had just decided it must be one of the dogs belonging to the Indians, when it was suddenly snatched from sight.

Every man on the "qui vive", the troopers dismounted and closed in on the spot. There sat a deformed Modoc henchman, supposedly on guard, but so intent on spreading out some camas root to dry that he was unaware of anyone's approach until the soldiers were upon him. He was trembling with fright as Captain Perry demanded that he give up his gun and tell Captain Jack to come out and surrender.

The hunchback did as he was told, and in a few minutes the Modoc Chief stepped boldly out on a shelf of rocks, took in the situation at a glance, then, with a gesture of resignation, dropped his rifle at his feet. As if it were a signal, two more warriors crept out of the rocks followed by five squaws and seven children.

Jack was dirty and ragged, shirt torn, old cavalry trousers in shreds, yet there was no sign of fear or trepidation as he limped painfully across the rocks with twenty gun barrels trained on him. A wave of admiration swept over the troopers as they recognized the essential heroism of this man who had successfully resisted them for so long.

Slowly, Kientepoos, Chief of the Modocs, walked into the circle of soldiers. Weak with hunger and fatigue, he sat down on a rock, with Captain Perry standing over him. Dignified, even in defeat, he studied the dusty yellow stripe on the officer's blue trousers as he raised his eyes unflinchingly to meet those of his captor.

"Jack's legs give out," was all he said.

CHAPTER XVII

GUARDHOUSE TO GALLOWS

NEWS of Captain Jack's capture was rushed by courier to Linkville, Fort Klamath, Yreka, and from the latter by telegraph to the presses of the country where it became the big front page item of the day. First to receive the message, however, was General Davis at Clear lake, who promptly dispatched orders to Fairchild's ranch to concentrate all troops and prisoners of war at the peninsula at Tule lake.

On June 1, the day after Captain Jack had surrendered, a strange procession rode into the headquarters camp at Applegate's ranch. The Warm Spring scouts rode in advance of the troops, chanting a strange, wild song of triumph. Captain Jack was mounted behind one of them, watching and listening to this celebration of his defeat with a stoical fortitude which gave no token by word, look or deed that it concerned him in the least. With a ceremonial flourish, the prisoners were turned over to General Davis, who ordered them placed under guard with other Modoc captives. Immediately, preparations were made for the troops to move to Tule lake. On June 3, they arrived at the place designated for the concentration camp.

Nowhere in the vicinity could a spot have been found more perfectly adapted for the detention of prisoners. The approach was over-shadowed by perpendicular, rocky bluffs which suggested the mighty towers and battlements of a feudal castle. The peninsula itself, a narrow neck of land, composed chiefly of coarse sand and myriads of tiny shells, connected the mainland with a long stretch of hill and bluff which otherwise would have formed an island. As the forces gathered from Clear lake and Fairchild's ranch, this strip became dotted with white army tents to provide shelter for the soldiers and about one hundred and sixty Modocs, most of whom were women and children.

On reaching the Tule lake camp, one of the first official acts Davis made was to order leg-shackles made for Captain Jack and Schonchin John. The two braves were distinctly apprehensive, for the first time, as they were led to the blacksmith shop under heavy guard. They could not, at first, comprehend what was to be done to them. When they finally were made to understand that they were to be chained together, they protested vigorously, insisting that their surrender had been made in good faith, and that under no circumstances would they attempt to escape. Orders were orders to the blacksmith, however, and when Captain Jack and Schonchin John realized their pleading was futile, they submitted in silence while the chains which bound them together were riveted.

That night, with only a few of the less important Modocs still at large, the Warm Springs Indians celebrated the end of the campaign by treating the camp to a fantastic exhibition, depicting in pantomime the outstanding scenes of the war. Its terrible and ludicrous happenings were reproduced with a veracity and color which was nothing short of spectacular; soldiers were surprised, slain, stripped; squaws were pictured toiling under heavy loads as the Modocs made their escape; Captain Jack was again captured. All this was accompanied by wild, plaintive songs, hoarse notes of war-drums and the eerie flickering of the camp-fire.

This was a brief interlude, however, in the more serious business at hand. General Davis went grimly about his duties, directing the erection of a scaffold for the purpose of hanging eight or ten of the ringleaders of the renegade band on the spot. Wagons were sent to the nearby mountains to secure timbers, and carpenters, under the direction of the quartermaster, were set to work.

As the Modocs watched the strange structure rise, their curiosity became aroused. "What for that thing they make?" Scarface asked a soldier.

"To hang Modocs," was the laconic reply.

A wave of consternation swept over the redskins as the word was passed swiftly from one to the other. Curly Head Doctor was the only one who took the news calmly. "I can beat that thing!" he boasted, and immediately set about "making medicine" for the purpose.

When the gallows were nearly completed, Captain Jack and Schonchin John were led away from the rest of the prisoners, their shackles clanking noisily as they walked. Great excitement gripped their tribesmen as a vision of ropes dangling from heavy beams flashed before them.

The two prisoners were noticeably disturbed, also, as they were taken to a spot near the scaffold where a man with a black cloth across his shoulders was tinkering with what they thought was a "big gun" mounted on three legs. Fully expecting to meet their death, they nevertheless stood stoically where they were placed, and watched the man duck down behind the machine and pull the black cloth over his head. Tensely they waited, but nothing occurred except a sharp click. The "big gun" had failed to go off.

When told it was all over and they could go back to their people, they seemed bewildered. Even when it was explained to them that they had simply had their pictures taken, they were as mystified as ever, but, obviously, relieved that they were not to die . . . yet.

The gallows were completed the next day, the ropes and traps tested and pronounced ready for duty. General Davis was waiting only for some of the prisoners and troopers from Fairchild's ranch to arrive before the execution . . . a task he recoiled from, yet considered his duty. The victims were to be the braves who had participated in the massacre of the peace commissioners, not excepting those who had tried to buy themselves off by turning traitor to their Chief. Davis was engaged in preparing a statement of the crimes they had committed when he heard the pounding of horses' hoofs. In a few seconds a dusty cavalryman rushed into Davis' tent.

"Five Modoc prisoners been killed, sir!" he gasped breathlessly, forgetting to salute in his excitement.

General Davis jumped to his feet. "Who by? Where?" he demanded.

"Over near Lost river, sir. Jim Fairchild, John's brother, was bringin' in a wagon load of 'em, all unarmed, some of 'em squaws and children, when two white men jumped out from the brush, stuck a gun to his head and forced him to the ground. Then they cut loose the mules from the wagon an' started shootin'!

"Is Fairchild all right?"

"Yes sir. But maybe he wouldn't be if our cavalry troop hadn't come along just when we did, 'cause he was mad enough to get himself in plenty of trouble!"

"Who were the two men . . . do you know?"

"Never seen 'em before, sir. They beat it you bet, when they seen us comin'."

"Did you try to arrest them?"

"No sir. We never had no orders to arrest white men."

"No orders! Hmm! Well, where are Fairchild and the prisoners now?"

"Comin' in, sir. They got the harness patched up and the cavalry troop's escortin' 'em."

General Davis dismissed the messenger and called his orderly. "As soon as Fairchild's party comes in, have the bugler blow the assembly call," he ordered. "The sooner we get this hanging business over with, the better."

He had no sooner resumed writing his statement than he was again interrupted . . . this time by a courier who handed him a dispatch from Washington, via Yreka.

"Congratulations on capture," he read. "Hold prisoners subject to further instructions."

Both relieved and chagrined, Davis tore up the papers on which he had been working, cancelled the instructions to his orderly, and threw all his energy into preparations for moving the whole camp to Fort Klamath, where better accommodations were to be had for the prisoners and troopers. The scaffold was left untried, with Curly Head Doctor triumphantly assuring his friends that he had "beat the death ropes" as he had promised.

The trip to the fort was uneventful except for an incident which occurred as the caravan of soldiers and captives was preparing to get under way early in the morning after the first night's camp. Nearly all of the Indians had taken their places in the wagons when the sharp crack of a pistol echoed through the still air. A moment later Scarface Charley came running up to General Davis and breathlessly reported that Curly Jack had shot and killed himself. Where he had secured the gun, no one knew. The soldiers lost no time in digging a shallow grave just a few feet from where the brave had fallen. He was buried unceremoniously and the wagon train moved on.

After two more days of arduous travel, the irregular amphitheatre of pines which surrounded Fort Klamath, came into view about sundown. that night, the troopers experienced the first taste of **civilized** comfort they had known for months; the captive Modocs, the first confinement within prison walls they had ever known.

The band was divided, the braves being placed in the guard-house, the squaws and children in the stockade. The parade grounds, centered by a tall flag-staff flying the stars and stripes, separated the two. The wooden building where the braves were held was divided into cells in which the head men of the tribe were locked, while the rest of the braves occupied one large bunk-lined room in common. Guards paced an unceasing beat, back and forth along the veranda at the front, which faced the open square. The stockade was a large enclosure which looked like a square corral, with the squaws and children giving the impression of frightened animals as they peered through the cracks between the vertical pine poles of which it was constructed.

While the prisoners were, with difficulty, adjusting

themselves to their new mode of living, the wheels which would determine their fate began to turn. General Davis received instructions from Washington to try, by court martial, the braves involved in the slaying of the peace commissioners, and accordingly, he appointed Major H. P. Curtis as judge-advocate and five other officers to act on the military commission.

A difference of opinion arose between Curtis and Davis as to whether those who had turned traitor to Captain Jack and assisted in his capture should be made to stand trial. Davis declared that he had made them no promises; that he had fully expected them to be treated on the same basis as the others. Major Curtis, however, pointed out that without their invaluable assistance, the renegade Chief might still be at large. Exercising his prerogative as judge-advocate, he decreed that they should not stand trial, nor even be considered under arrest.

As a result of this decision, four tents were pitched on the parade grounds near the stockade for the use of Bogus Charley, Steamboat Frank, Hooker Jim, Shacknasty Jim and their families. Scarface Charley was also allowed the freedom of the fort, but he did not join in the gambling and loud talk in which these four braves were habitually engaged. Instead, he could usually be found sitting by himself in gloomy silence.

As the day for the opening of the trial drew near, the assembly hall of the fort was converted into a court room. A long, narrow council table was placed in the center, with a bench for the prisoners at the right and a table for the newspaper reporters at the left. The only touch of color was provided by the flag which hung from a standard at one end of the hall.

The trial opened on July 4, 1873. The military

commission, resplendent in new uniforms, took their places at the center table, at the head of which sat Judge-Advocate Curtis. At his left was the court reporter and at his right, Frank and Winema Riddle, who had been sent for to act as interpreters and witnesses for the prosecution. A file of immaculately groomed soldiers, rifles tipped with shining bayonets, stood guard at each end of the room. There were no spectators allowed, except the four "Modoc bloodhounds" who lounged unfettered, near the door.

At ten o'clock the court convened and the officer of the day was sent to bring in the prisoners under guard. The six stolid-faced braves entered hesitantly through the door at the rear, their dark skin and shabby clothing contrasting sharply with the splendor of the military tribunal. Captain Jack and Schonchin John, still in shackles, sat down on the bench with Black Jim and Boston Charley, while the two others, Barncho and Slolux, squatted on the floor.

Members of the commission, the interpreters and the court reporter were duly sworn in and the prisoners asked if they wished to introduce counsel. Captain Jack replied that they knew of no one who would talk for the Modocs. They were then asked to stand as the charges preferred against them were read and interpreted, namely: murder and assault with intent to kill in violation of the laws of war, specifying the slaying of General E. R. S. Canby and Reverend Eleazar Thomas, and the attempt on the lives of A. B. Meacham and L. S. Dyer. To these accusations, each brave pleaded not guilty.

The formalities disposed of, the court proceeded to examine witnesses for the prosecution, including Frank and Winema Riddle and Mr. Dyer. Their testimony, which occupied the rest of that day, brought out nothing new and went unchallenged by the prisoners.

The next day, the trial continued with Shacknasty Jim, Steamboat Frank, Bogus Charley and Hooker Jim taking the stand against their fellow-tribesmen, each of them naming Captain Jack and Schonchin John as the instigators of the treacherous plot to assassinate the commissioners. William Faithful had been sworn in late that afternoon and was under examination when the door at the front of the courtroom opened and A. B. Meacham walked in unassumingly. The prisoners stared at him with incredulity written on their faces, for they had never been convinced that he had recovered from the wounds they had inflicted.

Meacham was called forward as a witness, but after a brief routine questioning, the court adjourned until the next morning. The prisoners, casting anxious glances at the man they believed dead, were remanded to the guardhouse. When they had gone, Meacham questioned the members of the commission.

"Have the prisoners no counsel?" he asked.

"They haven't been able to obtain any," he was told.

"Then why wasn't counsel appointed for them? It's only fair that both sides should be fully brought out."

"Well, we would have preferred to, but there's no one here who would accept such an appointment."

Meacham considered thoughtfully for a moment. "I don't have any desire to shield the prisoners, but I do think their side should be presented. Sooner than have it said that this was an ex parte trial, I'll appear as their counsel myself . . . with your consent."

The commission, although fairly dumfounded by his proposal, agreed that his services would be most welcome, but questioned whether he had the strength for such a task.

"Well, it's true I've none too much energy," he admitted. "It's only been three months since I was wounded, and during that time, I've traveled back and forth twice between here and Washington. At any rate, I'll see what the doctors think about it, and in the meantime, I'd like an interview with the prisoners."

This was readily arranged and a few minutes later, Captain Jack and Schonchin John were brought from their cell in the guardhouse to confront Meacham. They came slowly, with eyes glued on the man before them. Schonchin took hold of his arm and pressed it slightly, then grunted his conviction that it really was Meacham and that he was actually alive.

Captain Jack, after his first diffidence had worn off, was eager to talk about the trial. When asked why he didn't get a lawyer to talk for him, he replied, "Everyone against Modocs. Anyhow, lawyer do no good. He no understand this thing. White man has many voices. He tell one side but not the other."

"Why not tell it yourself, then?" Meacham suggested.

Captain Jack looked down at his shackles. "I cannot talk with chains on legs," he said in a low voice. "My heart is not strong when I feel chains on legs. You can talk strong talk. You talk for me."

Meacham promised he would try to see that the case for the Modocs was presented and left to consult the army surgeons in regard to offering himself as counsel. There was but one answer . . . that if he did so, the exertion might cost him his life.

On the fourth day of the trial, the testimony for the prosecution was completed and, in the absence of anyone to legally represent them, the prisoners were given an opportunity to speak for themselves. When Captain Jack was informed that he could make a statement, he rose hesitantly to his feet, glanced down at his chains, then pulled himself together with a visible effort as he deliberately scanned the court. He began to speak in a low, suppressed tone, with Winema interpreting his words:

"When I was a boy I had it in my heart to be friend to white man. I was their friend until my own people turned my heart when they forced me to kill soldier ty-ee, Canby. You palefaces did not conquer me . . . my own braves conquered me. Some of them are here today, free men, while I am in irons. They are the ones who wanted to kill peace-mans. I fought against it. But they taunted and threatened me until I had to say yes. If I had only known they would then betray me like they did, you would not have me here to-day with chains on my legs and smiles on your faces."

The Modoc chieftain's voice rose, grew heated as he continued: "You white people drove me from mountain to mountain, from valley to valley, like wounded deer. At last you have got me here. You say I am bad man. You say I killed Canby. Yes, I did kill him, but I see no crime in my heart. My heart is not bad. The ones most guilty are the ones now free. If white man's law not crooked like snake, they would be here in chains along with these others.

"I am ashamed to die with rope around my neck. I wanted to die on battlefield with gun in my hand. But I am not afraid. I only think of my people and hope you don't treat them bad on account of what wrongs I did. If government will give them fair chance, they will prove worthy of it.

"But do we Indians stand chance to be treated fair by white people? I say no! I know it! Paleface can shoot Indian any time he wants, whether in war or peace. Can you tell me where one white man has been punished for killing Modoc? No! You cannot tell me!

"Now here I am . . . killed one man, after I had been fooled by him many times and forced to do the act by my own warriors. The law says, hang him. He is nothing but an Indian, anyhow. We can kill him any time for nothing, but this time he has done something, so hang him! Let me hang, then! I am not afraid to die. I will show you how a Modoc can die. I am done."

When Captain Jack sat down a profound silence enveloped the courtroom for several moments, mute evidence to the impression his speech had made. The commissioners immediately regained their brusque manner, however, and the judge-advocate called for any others who wished to speak to do so. Slolux, Barncho, Black Jim, Boston Charley and Schonchin Jim each said what little they could in their own defense, either protesting their innocence or facing their fate with bravado as did Boston Charley. The one thing they had in common was indignation that the "traitor" braves had not been made to stand trial.

When each had spoken, the unanimous verdict of "guilty as charged" was pronounced. Without further ceremony, the court was adjourned, the trial ended. There was no doubt as to what the sentence would be, although announcement of it was delayed pending approval from Washington, which was received in the following communication, dated August 22, 1873:

"Executive Office.

"The foregoing sentences (to be hanged by the neck until dead) in the cases of Captain Jack, Schonchin John, Black Jim, Boston Charley, Barncho and Slolux, Modoc Indian prisoners, are hereby approved; and it is ordered that the sentences in said cases be carried into execution by proper military authority, under the orders of the Secretary of War, on the third day of October, eighteen hundred and seventy-three.

"U. S. Grant,
"President."

During the interval between the trial and the pronouncement of sentence, day dragged after day as the Modoc captives suffered increasingly from their unaccustomed confinement, which the blistering sun turned into a form of slow torture. The only relief from monotony they were afforded were the infrequent occasions when the braves were allowed to visit their families in the stockade, or when the women and children were allowed a few minutes with their husbands and fathers in the guardhouse. But these periods only intensified their nostalgia for the expansive distances of their Lost river country, to a point where many of them longed for the day to arrive which would bring them release . . . even if that release must come through death.

Slowly July and August gave way to the Indian summer of September. Golden, mellow days they were, with a suggestion of tang in the air which revived in the condemned braves the desire to live. Yet as each day passed, the approach of the time they were to die was heralded by the pounding of hammers and the rasp of saws as construction of the scaffold was begun.

The site selected for it was in an open plat of meadow near the guardhouse where the prisoners could watch it rise, step by step. The carpenters first set to work on a rectangular platform about thirty feet long, eight feet wide and nine feet high, down the length of which ran a long, narrow trap. Thirteen steps formed an approach to it on one side, while at the ends, sturdy posts were anchored to support a rugged crossbeam about nine feet above the floor of the platform. At last the day came when six heavy ropes were suspended from the beam . . . and the gruesome gallows were ready for use.

On that same day, the attention of Hooker, Steamboat, Shacknasty and Bogus was attracted to the strange activities of a group of men near the guard-house. The four braves leaned on a fence and watched in silence as the workers carefully measured the ground with a tapeline, then drove small pegs around which they strung heavy cord until six small plots were enclosed. When the men took up shovels and started to dig, the curiosity of the Indians gained the upper hand.

"What for you do that?" Bogus demanded of one of them.

"Making a new home for Jack and his friends," the grave-digger replied, and tossed another shovel-full of dirt aside.

Involuntarily, the braves glanced furtively toward the guard-house . . . and straight into the eyes of Boston Charley, who was peering between the bars of his cell window. The look on the prisoner's face was ample evidence that he had missed nothing. He muttered a few words over his shoulder which brought the others to their windows, where they stood for a moment watching the digging of their own graves, then quickly turned away.

That afternoon, the men confined in the prison cells received a visit which definitely confirmed their fast-growing realization that the end was not far off. Their visitors were General Wheaton, arrayed in full uniform; a white-haired Catholic priest; the tall, dignified Captain Oliver Applegate and the swarthy Klamath scout, Dave Hill. As these men entered the guard-house accompanied by a heavy guard of troopers, they presented a sharp contrast to the ragged Modoc prisoners who gathered around them.

The windows were darkened by faces of the curious, eager to see and to hear what was going on, as General Wheaton requested the chaplain to officially inform the prisoners of the decision of the President. In a few words which fell upon a breathless silence, the reluctant priest told them that the hour of ten o'clock the next morning had been set as the time of execution for those whom the court had convicted. As Captain Applegate and Dave Hill interpreted the words, the Modoc chief appeared for a moment to be completely unmanned. Then he partially regained his composure, and spoke in a voice so low as to be scarcely audible.

"I hear your words," he said. "I know their meaning. When I look in my heart I see no bad blood. But if the Great White Father says I must die, I will die as a Modoc should . . . like a man."

The other condemned braves were deeply affected. Schonchin John's face twitched and his fingers worked convulsively; Black Jim paled, but the sinister, scornful smile never left his face; Boston Charley sat chewing on a wad of tobacco, trying to appear indifferent, but his hands were trembling; Barncho's head sank to his chest, Slolux breathed heavily as he gripped the bench on which he was sitting. In a few minutes, however, all except Schonchin had lapsed into their usual stolidity and showed no further emotion.

Each brave was given an opportunity to speak, after which the kindly chaplain talked to them quietly, trying to give them strength to meet the coming ordeal. His voice was tremulous as he closed his remarks with a brief prayer, then covered his face with his hands as he gave way to sobs of pity. He recovered his self-possession, however, as each of the white men shook hands with the Indians who were to die, and left them alone with their thoughts.

About five o'clock, the wives and children of the braves were allowed to visit the convicted Indians for the last time. The squaws filled the air with wails of lamentation which could be heard all over the fort, as they clung to their men with a tenacity born of desperation. Other squaws, whose loved ones were not among the condemned, flocked around, asking with blank faces if Captain Jack was to be killed. The wailing and moaning continued unabated until the distraught women were taken back to the stockade. Then they lapsed into a period of silence and despair. But as darkness fell, they again became loud in their expressions of anguish, and few persons in all the encampment slept that night.

A golden haze softened the rugged outlines of the mountains around Fort Klamath, as morning dawned, revealing a large group of people who had already assembled in the meadow around the gallows. As the sun rose higher, they continued to come until they numbered several hundred. Among them were practically all of the Klamaths, wearing self-satisfied expressions on their faces; a few Modocs who had avoided trouble with the whites by staying on the reservation at Yainax; and dozens of settlers who had driven wagons or ridden horseback from far and near to witness the spectacle.

The crowd was patient and orderly until the bugle rang out the assembly call at 9:00 o'clock. Then they began to push and elbow each other, climbing onto fences, wagons and even into trees in their eagerness to catch the first glimpse of the condemned Modocs. They watched intently as a battalion of soldiers formed on the parade ground and stood rigidly at attention, while the officer of the day entered the guardhouse, and reappeared with the condemned Indians.

Awaiting the prisoners was a wagon loaded with four pine boxes and drawn by a four-horse team. Surrounded by a heavy guard, the six braves were assisted into the wagon where they sat down on the empty coffins for the short ride to the gallows. They were all dressed in old blue army trousers and blouses except Captain Jack, who wore a bright checkered shirt with a blanket thrown over his shoulders.

At a signal from General Wheaton, the band played the opening strains of the "Dead March", to the accompaniment of which the column of soldiers marched slowly toward the scaffold, followed by the prisoners and their guard.

In these few minutes, the prisoners lost nothing of their surroundings. They heard the cries of their women and children, and observed that the stockade commanded a direct view of the death-ropes. These condemned men caught a glimpse of Scarface Charley, sitting alone with his back to the crowd, his face buried in his hands. They saw the four braves who had hunted them down, occupying a privileged spot where they could see the death struggles of their victims, unobstructed. But the thing which made the deepest impression on the doomed braves was the discrepancy between the six open graves, the six dangling ropes and the four coffins on which they sat. Could it be that two of them were not to die? And if so, which two? A new hope leapt up in the heart of each of them.

As the procession drew near the gallows, the crowd fell back, the column of soldiers separated, right and left, and the wagon passed between the two files and stopped at the foot of the thirteen steps. General Wheaton created a sensation in the crowd as he stepped forward and motioned Barncho and Slolux to stay where they were, while the other four men were helped to the ground. An expectant hush prevailed, broken by the sharp ring of steel on steel as the prisoners' chains were severed with a cold chisel and the four braves mounted the steps to the platform.

Captain Jack and Black Jim appeared unmoved as the braves were each assigned a place under a rope. Boston Charley took one last chew of tobacco and spit contemptuously; Schonchin John wavered, stumbled and almost fell. An adjutant followed them to the platform and read the official order for the execution in a clear, firm voice which fell upon the ears of an awed assemblage. When this had been interpreted so all could understand, he drew another piece of paper from his pocket, instructed Barncho and Slolux to stand, and he read the following:

"Executive Office,
"Washington, D. C.,
"September 10, 1873.
"The executive order dated August 22, 1873, approving the sentence of death of certain Modoc Indian

prisoners, is hereby modified in the case of Barncho and Slolux; and the sentence in said cases is commuted to imprisonment for life. Alcatraz island, harbor of San Francisco, California, is designated as the place of confinement.

"U. S. Grant,
"President."

As the interpreter made clear the meaning of the words Barncho slowly removed his cap and Slolux wiped his eyes on the sleeve of his blouse. When it was over the two young braves limply resumed their seats on the coffins of their less fortunate comrades.

From then on, things moved swiftly. The arms and legs of the condemned men were bound, the ropes carefully adjusted around their necks, black hoods placed over their heads. A tense corporal gripped the handle of a sharp axe, jaw set, knuckles white, as he stood ready to cut the rope which held the trap. The chaplain offered up a brief prayer for those who were to die. As he made the sign of the cross there was a flash of polished steel, the taut jerk of the ropes . . . and four convulsed bodies dangled in the air.

CHAPTER XVIII

A TRIBE IN EXILE

FOLLOWING the execution, the four bodies were taken from the scaffold and placed in the coffins which were lowered without ceremony into the graves which had been dug for them. The two unused excavations were filled and their intended occupants, Barncho and Slolux, sent to serve out their lives in Alcatraz prison in San Francisco bay.

Once more the stockmen and ranchers of the Lost river country breathed easily as they went about their business without fear . . . but at what a cost! Close to a million dollars in the currency of the day had been poured into the campaign against the Modocs. Hundreds of soldiers had marched as far as two hundred miles, and fought side by side with volunteers and Warm Springs Indians to subdue this band of fifty-three warriors, entrenched in the Lava Beds, defending what they thought was their right to a home in their Lost river country.

Seventeen of these braves were now dead, having succumbed to bullets, shell fire or the gallows. Yet for each of these redskins, the government had sacrificed the lives of at least a dozen men. During the whole campaign, the total number of soldiers, volunteers and civilians killed by the Modocs ran into the hundreds . . . in fact, almost as many as were killed in battle on the American side in the whole Spanish-American war!

The survivors of the Modoc band were herded into wagons and taken to Redding, California, the nearest railroad, from whence they were shipped to Quawpaw agency, Indian Territory, Oklahoma. There the remnants of this blood-stained, broken people mourned the ignominious death of their Chief and lived out their lives in a land of exile.

BIBLIOGRAPHY

Bancroft, H. H.—Volume II, p. 555, in *History of Oregon*. San Francisco: History Company, 1886.

Brady, C. J.—Page 227 in *Northwestern Fights and Fighters*. New York: Doubleday-Page & Co., 1907.

Executive Documents, First Session, 43rd Congress. Printed by Order of the House of Representatives, 1873-1874. Vol. 9, Nos. 58 to 122 inclusive. Washington, D. C.: Government Printing Office, 1874.

Executive Documents, Second Session, 43rd Congress. Printed by Order of the House of Representatives, 1874-1875. Vol. 12, Nos. 45 to 78 inclusive. Washington, D. C.: Government Printing Office, 1875.

Gaston, Joseph—Chapter XIV, pp. 415-420 in *The Centennial History of Oregon*, Vol. 1. Chicago: S. J. Clarke Publishing Co., 1912.

Gatschet, A. S.—*The Klamath Indians of Southwestern Oregon*. Washington, D. C.: Government Printing Office, 1890.

Grover, Governor—*Report to General Schofield on the Modoc War*. Salem, Oregon: State Printing Office, 1874. (950.5, Or. 32, State Law Library.)

Meacham, A. B.—pp. 74-83, 323-325, in *Annual Report of the Commissioner of Indian Affairs to the Secretary of the Interior for the Year* 1873. Washington, D. C.: Government Printing Office, 1874.

Meacham, A. B.—Page 289-664 in *Wigwam and Warpath*. Boston: John P. Dale & Company, 1875.

Meacham, A. B.—*Winema (The Woman Chief) and Her People*. Hartford, 1876.

Miller, John F.—*Report to Governor Grover* (From Headquarters, District of Lakes, camp near Van Bremer's ranch, dated January 20, 1873.) Salem, Oregon: State Printing Office, 1874. (950.5, Or. 32 State Law Library.)

Nixon, Robert—*The Modoc War: A Brief and Authentic History*. Yreka, Calif.: (Manuscript).

Riddle, Jeff C.—*Indian History of the Modoc War*. Riddle, 1914.

Ross, General John E.—*Reports to Governor Grover*. Jacksonville, dated February 20, July 4, 1873. Salem, Oregon: State Printing Office, 1874. (950.5, Or. 32, State Law Library.)

Shaver, F. A.—Chapter III, pp. 942-967 and "Incident of the Modoc War", p. 1091, in *History of Central Oregon*. Spokane: Western Historical Publishing Co., 1905.

Turner, William M.—Page 21, *Overland Monthly*. San Francisco, July, 1873.

Wheaton, Lieut.-Col. Frank—Extract From General Field Order Number I, headquarters District of Lakes, camp near Crawley's ranch. Dated December 20, 1872, January 12, 1873. Salem, Ore.: State Printing Office.

Yreka Journal, published weekly at Yreka, Siskiyou country, California, by Robert Nixon. File of issues for 1872, 1873.

Yreka Union, official paper for Siskiyou and Klamath counties, published weekly at Yreka, California, by William Irwin. File of issues for 1872, 1873.

THE AUTHOR

DORIS Palmer Payne has been a "northwesterner" a comparatively short time, but she has more than compensated for not being a pioneer daughter by the avidity with which she has absorbed the spirit and feeling of the Old West. Claiming Santa Monica, California, as her birthplace, and the University of California, Berkeley, as her Alma Mater, she moved still farther north in 1932, locating in Klamath Falls, Oregon, where she now makes her home. *Captain Jack, Modoc Renegade* is Mrs. Payne's first book, her other writing being in the newspaper and magazine fields.

Both Mrs. Payne and her husband, Frank A. Payne, have been intensely interested in the Lava Beds country. Mr. Payne has gained a widespread reputation for his outstanding collection of arrowheads and other artifacts of the Modoc Indians. The finding, preserving and mounting of these relics of primitive workmanship, which number in the thousands, is the major hobby of Mr. and Mrs. Payne and their two children.

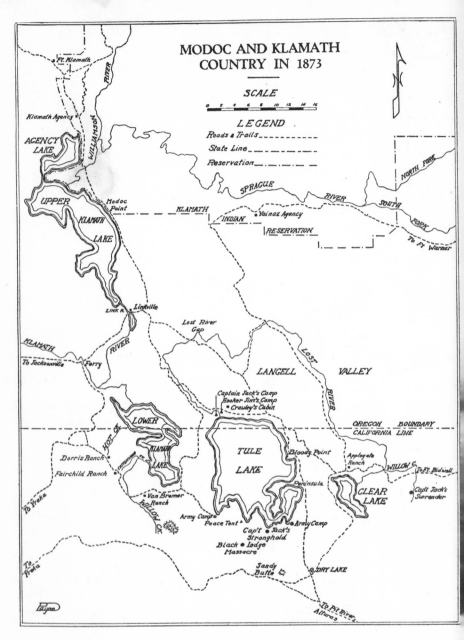

MODOC AND KLAMATH
COUNTRY IN 1873

SCALE

LEGEND

Roads & Trails _____
State Line _ _ _ _ _ _ _ _
Reservation _ . _ . _ . _ .

Ft. Klamath

Klamath Agency

AGENCY
LAKE

WILLIAMSON RIVER

NORTH FORK

UPPER

KLAMATH

LAKE

Modoc Point

KLAMATH

Yainax Agency

INDIAN

RESERVATION

SPRAGUE RIVER

SOUTH FORK

To Ft. Warner

LINK R. *Linkville*

Lost River Gap

KLAMATH

RIVER

To Jacksonville

Ferry

LANGELL

VALLEY

LOST RIVER

Captain Jack's Camp
Hooker Jim's Camp
Crawley's Cabin

OREGON BOUNDARY
CALIFORNIA LINE

LOWER

KLAMATH

LAKE

Hot Cr.

Dorris Ranch

Fairchild Ranch

Cottonwood

To Yreka

Van Bremer Ranch

WILLOW CR.

Army Camp
Peace Tent

To Yreka

Black Ledge Massacre

Cap't Jack's Stronghold

Sandy Butte

TULE

LAKE

Bloody Point

Peninsula

Army Camp

Applegate Ranch

WILLOW C.

To Ft. Bidwell

CLEAR

LAKE

Cap't Jack's Surrender

DRY LAKE

To Pit River Alturas

Payne

*This rugged, high-mountain country of Southern Oregon
and Northern California, formed by volcanoes now
extinct, abounded in lakes, forests and sagebrush-covered valleys.*